THE WORLD'S GREATEST INVESTMENT IDEAS

31 secrets and strategies that will make you a world-class investor

Published by Stansberry & Associates Investment Research.

INTRODUCTION

Dear reader,

You hold in your hands some of the most valuable information in the world.

You hold the wisdom learned from thousands of books... and gained from hundreds of thousands of hours of practice. You hold the most valuable ideas you can learn from the world's best businessmen and investors.

I realize those are bold statements. So let me explain where they come from...

My name is Brian Hunt. I'm the Editor in Chief of the world's largest independent financial newsletter publishing firm, Stansberry & Associates Investment Research.

Founded in 1999 by Porter Stansberry, Stansberry & Associates has over 400,000 paid-up subscribers in more than 100 countries.

We've become such a large and trusted research organization for a few reasons...

One, we accept no kickbacks, banking fees, or commissions for anything we write. We serve our customers' interests and no one else's. We are 100% independent and unbiased. Two, we have an extraordinary record of getting big calls right... and helping investors learn the keys to safe, successful investing.

The biggest reason, however, is people. Our organization has attracted some of the world's brightest minds... by employing them directly... or by maintaining good working relationships with them.

For example, we've cultivated a friendship with Van Simmons, who is an undisputed authority on collectibles and precious metals. When Van speaks, billionaires listen. We also stay in close contact with Rick Rule, one of the top natural resource financiers in the world. Rick has become a very wealthy man because of his unconventional investment strategies.

On staff, Stansberry & Associates has people like Dr. David Eifrig. "Doc," as we call him, is a former Goldman Sachs trading executive and a board-eligible eye surgeon. He's also one of America's most trusted retirement experts. He's a walking encyclopedia of valuable information on health, wealth, and life in general. He's also one of my closest friends.

I also like to think we're "close" with people who are long gone by now. We've all read many books from many people. We've studied the ideas and writings of legendary businessmen like Andrew Carnegie, J. Paul Getty, and Benjamin Graham.

As for modern-day legends, we're also intellectual disciples of Warren Buffett, Jim Rogers, and John Templeton.

This book is a collection of interviews gleaned from all of these sources. It consists of 31 interviews with people who work at Stansberry & Associates... and with our most knowledgeable friends and contacts.

We came up with some of these ideas on our own. Some of them come from investment legends like Warren Buffett. To paraphrase, if we can see further, it is because we stand on the shoulders of giants.

These interviews are relatively short. You won't spend hours digging into one single topic. The goal of this book is to expose you to more than two dozen of the world's best ideas on producing wealth, preserving wealth, and growing wealth.

Some of these interviews focus on behaviors of successful wealth-builders. Some of them focus on specific investment techniques. Some simply focus on useful ways of looking at the world.

I've spent the past 17 years studying the art of wealth-building and investment. I have classic books like *The Richest Man in Babylon*, *Investment Biker*, and *One Up on Wall Street* in my head and on my bookshelf. I've met, read, or worked with almost every investment guru in the world. And these are the very best ideas my colleagues and I have ever found.

In this book, you'll learn the most powerful investment secrets in the world... how to identify a great business... how to get a big raise at work... why you should never retire in the conventional sense... the greatest financial gift you can give to your children... a simple way to make a fortune in natural resources... and many more brilliant ideas.

This book is "condensed" wisdom. It's full of ideas I wish I knew when I started out as an investor.

I hope you enjoy them... and I hope they help you achieve personal and financial freedom.

Regards,

Brian Hunt

CONTENTS

BIOGRAPHIES

PORTER STANSBERRY

Porter Stansberry is the editor of *Stansberry's Investment Advisory*, where Porter predicts the most promising emerging trends and the most influential economic forces affecting the market. He is also the editor of *Stansberry Alpha*, which uses one trading technique in the options market. And he is the host of Stansberry Radio, a weekly broadcast that has quickly become one of the most popular online financial radio shows.

Prior to founding Stansberry & Associates Investment Research in 1999, Porter was the first American editor of the *Fleet Street Letter*, the world's oldest English-language financial newsletter.

At S&A, Porter oversees over a dozen of the best editors and analysts in the business, who do an exhaustive amount of real-world, independent research. Together, his group has visited hundreds of publicly traded companies to bring S&A subscribers the safest, most profitable investment ideas in the world, no matter what's happening in the markets.

BRIAN HUNT

Brian Hunt is the Editor in Chief of Stansberry & Associates.

Since 2007, he has managed dozens of S&A's investment newsletters and trading advisories, helping make S&A one of the largest financial publishers in the world.

Brian is a successful private trader and frequently contributes to *Growth Stock Wire*, *DailyWealth*, and the *S&A Digest*. He is the co-founder of *DailyWealth Trader*, one of the world's most popular and most highly-regarded trading advisories.

Brian is also the co-author of the book *High Income Retirement: How to Safely Earn 12%-20% Income Streams on Your Savings*.

DR. STEVE SJUGGERUD

Dr. Steve Sjuggerud is the editor of *True Wealth*, which focuses on safe, unique alternative investments overlooked by Wall Street. He is also the editor of *True Wealth Systems*, which distills decades of Steve's investing experience into three dozen computer trading models.

Prior to joining S&A in 2001, Steve was a stockbroker, vice president of a global mutual fund, and head of a hedge fund. He has been quoted by the *Wall Street Journal, Barron's,* and the *Washington Post.* He also co-authored *Safe Strategies for Financial Freedom*, a best-selling book on investment strategies. And he holds a doctorate in finance.

DR. DAVID EIFRIG

Dr. David Eifrig Jr. is the editor of *Retirement Millionaire*, which shows readers how to live a millionaire lifestyle on less money than you'd imagine possible. He is also the editor of *Income Intelligence*, a monthly investment advisory which shows investors how to expertly time their purchases to maximize their returns.

Before joining Stansberry & Associates in 2008, "Doc" worked in arbitrage and trading groups with major Wall Street investment banks, including Goldman Sachs, Chase Manhattan, and Yamaichi in Japan. In 1995, he retired from Wall Street, went to UNC-Chapel Hill medical school, and became a board-eligible eye surgeon.

He has been interviewed by *The Energy Report* and *Everything Financial Radio* and has appeared on Fox News.

DAN FERRIS

Dan Ferris is the editor of *Extreme Value*, which focuses on great businesses trading at steep discounts.

Dan joined Stansberry & Associates in 2000. He has been featured several times in *Barron's, USA Today,* the *Value Investing Letter,* and numerous financial radio programs around the country.

JEFF CLARK

Jeff Clark is the editor of the *S&A Short Report*, which focuses on short-term option trading. He's also the editor of *S&A Pro Trader,* which shows readers safe, sophisticated option-trading techniques.

Prior to joining S&A in 2005, Jeff was a longtime S&A subscriber and president and chief executive officer of an independent, San Francisco-based brokerage house and private money-management firm. Jeff also served as a consultant to one of the country's largest options market-making firms, developed the curricula for an international MBA program, and founded an investor education firm.

JOHN DOODY

John Doody is the founder and editor of *Gold Stock Analyst*, which features his proprietary gold-stock valuing system. From 2001-2010, his "Top 10" list of gold stocks returned 1,360%.

Prior to launching *Gold Stock Analyst*, John received a BA in Economics from Columbia, an MBA in finance, and a PhD in economics from Boston University. He was an economics professor for almost two decades.

But for the past 40 years, John has been studying and analyzing gold stocks. His opinion on these stocks is so respected, he has been profiled by *Barron's* several times, quoted in *The Financial Times*, and is frequently interviewed on CNBC. He counts several of the world's best-known gold funds and investment managers among his subscribers.

DOUG CASEY

Doug Casey is the chairman of Casey Research, a financial publishing firm specializing in commodity and natural resource investing.

Doug wrote the book on profiting from periods of economic turmoil: his book *Crisis Investing* spent multiple weeks as No. 1 on the *New York Times* bestseller list and became the best selling financial book of 1980. Doug is also the author of *Strategic Investing* and *The International Man*, one of the most well-known books on financial and personal opportunities outside America.

He has been a featured guest on hundreds of radio and TV shows, including David Letterman, Merv Griffin, Charlie Rose, Phil Donahue, Regis Philbin, Maury Povich, NBC News, and CNN. And he has been the topic of numerous features in periodicals and newspapers such as *Time, Forbes, People,* and the *Washington Post.*

MARK FORD

Mark Ford is the wealth coach of *The Palm Beach Letter*, which provides useful advice about building wealth, living well, and investing.

Over the last 30 years, Mark has built a reputation as one of the country's foremost experts on wealth building. A self-made millionaire, Mark knows all the tricks in the book for getting rich. He's a serial entrepreneur who has built hundreds of businesses... and a huge personal fortune. Mark is also a *New York Times* and *Wall Street Journal* best selling author... with hit books such as *Seven Years to Seven Figures, Automatic Wealth,* and *Ready, Fire, Aim: Zero to $100 Million in No Time Flat.*

JUSTIN FORD

Justin Ford is the President of Pax Properties, LLC, a diversified real estate company offering brokerage, mortgage, property management, and investment services in South Florida. With investors, Pax also owns and operates more than 100 rental units for its own portfolio.

Mr. Ford counts several Stansberry & Associates investment advisors among his investors. He's also the creator of *Justin Ford's C.A.P. Strategy: Bubble-Proof Real Estate Investing for Lifelong Cash Flow*. This educational course shows regular investors how to safely build huge wealth with conservative real estate strategies. You can learn more about this excellent course at http://capcashflow.com/.

RICK RULE

Rick Rule is the founder and chairman of Global Resource Investments, now a member of the Sprott Group of companies. Sprott Global Resource Investments provides investment advice and management, as well as brokerage services to high-net-worth individuals, institutional investors, and corporate entities worldwide.

Rick began his career in the securities business in 1974. He is a well-recognized expert in mining, energy, water, forest products, infrastructure, and agriculture. He has also financed several of the most important resource companies in the world. Rick is a frequent speaker at industry conferences and is often interviewed on numerous radio, television, print, and online media outlets, including Business News Network, CNBC, and King World News.

VAN SIMMONS

Van Simmons is the president of David Hall Rare Coins, one of the nation's largest rare-coin dealers.

Van is one of the most knowledgeable minds in the world on coins, stamps, and just about any other collectible you can think of. He has been a rare-coin collector since age 12 and a rare-coin dealer since 1979. As one of the founders of Professional Coin Grading Service (PCGS), the largest rare-coin grading service in the world, he has helped revolutionize the rare-coin market.

TOM DYSON

Tom Dyson is the publisher of *Common Sense Publishing,* which provides useful advice about building wealth, living well, and investing.

Tom graduated from the University of Nottingham, in the United Kingdom. He's a member of the Chartered Institute of Management Accountants, one of Britain's top accounting bodies. He has also worked for bond trading desks at Salomon Brothers and Citigroup.

LONG-TERM STOCK INVESTMENT

VALUING A STOCK AS A PRIVATE BUSINESS OWNER WOULD

When you buy a stock, do you see it as a piece of paper you're hoping to "flip" to someone at a higher price?

Or do you take a better approach... like the one advocated by investors like Warren Buffett?

This approach will instantly give you an advantage over the overwhelming majority of investors in the stock market. It's an excellent way to improve your long-term results.

If you're interested in making more money from stocks with less effort – and sleeping soundly at night while you do – this idea is for you. It is explained by Stansberry & Associates' Senior Analyst Dan Ferris, who is one of the top stock analysts in the world...

Stansberry & Associates: What does it mean to value a stock as a business? How does it differ from the way most investors think about investing?

Dan Ferris: Let's start by considering what a stock actually is. In simple terms, a share of stock represents a share of an actual business.

But as Warren Buffett says, most people tend to think of a stock as a ticker symbol with a squiggly line attached. Most people think it's easier to look at a stock chart and try to predict whether its price will go up or down, than it is to understand the underlying business. But the truth is, almost nobody is good at this. It takes an extremely rare individual who can do it with enough consistency to make money.

Some professional and dedicated part-time traders succeed by buying and selling stocks using short-term strategies. But the overwhelming majority of investors would make a lot more money – and lose a lot less – if they learned to approach stocks the way they'd approach ownership in a business.

You're much more likely to find a business that's simple enough to fully understand than you are to consistently predict where the price of a stock is going next.

S&A: What are the benefits of approaching investing this way?

Ferris: There are a number of benefits. Several of the world's greatest investors have shown this approach is one of the simplest, safest, and most consistent ways to make money in stocks. But perhaps even more important is the peace of mind it offers. Let me give you an example...

Suppose there are two investors who are buying stock. For the sake of this example, let's even assume they're both buying stock in the same company, XYZ.

Investor A approaches investing as a business owner and does a little homework on the underlying business. He sees company XYZ is a wonderful business trading at a good price, and he buys a size-able position.

Investor B is like most people and decides to buy XYZ without any real understanding of the underlying business. Maybe he saw the stock being touted on CNBC, heard this or that famous investor was buying it, or has a friend who made a lot of money in it.

If that stock goes up, both investors will probably be feeling good about their decision. But what if the stock suddenly falls 5%, 10%, or more? Or the market experiences a serious correction that takes most stocks down with it?

Investor A is much more likely to sleep well at night. He knows he bought a quality business and he knows he paid a good price for it. He knows the fluctuations in the share price have nothing to do with the underlying business. In fact, he may actually be happy to see the price fall – as Warren Buffett likes to say – because it will allow him to buy more shares or reinvest his dividends at a better price.

On the other hand, Investor B would probably be concerned. He has no idea what the underlying business is actually worth or what a fair price for it is. He only knows that he's lost money. He's probably wondering whether it will be a 5% correction or a 30% crash, and whether he should sell now or wait it out.

The fact is, you can't know those things in any kind of reliable manner. But you can know that great businesses consistently make money through good times and bad. And you can have a lot of certainty that over the long run you will be rewarded as a shareholder.

Just look at the history of the 20th Century... What calamity didn't happen in the 20th Century? We had two World Wars and a handful of smaller ones, a Great Depression, and great inflation. All the gold in the country was seized by the government, the dollar was taken off the gold standard, and we had 50%-90% marginal tax rates for many of those years. Yet over the century, the Dow Jones Industrial Average soared 1,500,000%.

Of course, you could argue that companies would have done even better without those government-created problems. But the point is, business trumped politics, wars, the economy, and inflation. There are never any guarantees in the stock market. But betting on great businesses was always the right thing to do over the last 100 years. And there is a very high probability that you'll do well buying the greatest businesses over the next 100 years.

S&A: How does an investor begin valuing stocks like a business owner?

Ferris: The first step is as simple as changing your thinking... It's deciding you won't buy a stock unless you can understand its business, it looks attractive, and it's reasonably priced.

Most folks would intuitively understand this if they were buying an actual business outright, but they seldom make the connection when buying stocks.

The first thing you'll notice when you begin thinking this way is, very few stocks are likely to meet those criteria. When you really understand what you're buying, you'll tend to be much more selective and gravitate toward great businesses.

S&A: Are there any simple ways to identify a great business?

Ferris: There are a few clues that great businesses leave behind. The easiest one to identify is a profit margin of consistent thickness over many years, even if it's a thin profit margin.

For example, Wal Mart's net profit margin is thin, around 3%. But it's a very consistent 3%. It's in the 3% range every year like clockwork. Most great businesses earn consistent profit margins.

Consistent margins tell you that something special is going on there. That business has been able to extract that profit out of the market because it's doing something that people really want year after year after year... And it has positioned itself in the marketplace so that it can keep doing it.

Another big clue of a great business is consistent free cash flow generation. That's a sign that the business doesn't require all kinds of expensive reinvestment year after year. It means the business can invest relatively little of that cash profit and put the rest toward things like paying out dividends, buying back shares, or making new investments in the future. A business gains a great deal of flexibility when it's able to generate a lot of free cash flow.

A third clue is a history of dividend payments that rise every single year for many years on end. Not all great businesses have this trait, but many of them do... so it's something to look for.

There are obviously more, but these are the big ones that most great businesses share.

S&A: Once you've identified a great business, how do you determine if it's trading at a good price? How do you value the business?

Ferris: There are two primary ways to value a business. One is by net worth, and the other one is by profit generation.

Net worth is calculated the same way you would do it for yourself. If you want to find out what your net worth is, you add up all your cash and all your assets, like your house, your cars, etc. Then you subtract everything you owe – things like your mortgage, your credit cards, and your car loans – and that difference is your net worth.

You can do the same thing with a company. You can look at a company's balance sheet and assign a value to its cash and other assets, add them all up, subtract what it owes – debt and other liabilities – and you get its net worth.

This is a simple example. This calculation can get rather complicated, depending on the business. Sometimes, assets have to be revalued, for example, if the company owns a bunch of land that it paid very little for many years ago that's worth much more now. But the basic idea is the same.

This measure of value is best-suited for asset-heavy businesses or strict value investing situations – where you're buying $1 worth of assets for a significant discount and waiting for the market to fairly value it. Fair valuations will vary significantly, depending on the industry and the situation.

The other way to value a business is based on profit generation, or how much free cash flow the company produces. This tends to be a better measure of value for really great businesses... businesses that you're confident are going to make more money next year, five years from now, and 20 years from now.

We can look to history for a benchmark for valuing these great businesses. When companies have bought out or taken over really great businesses in the past – for example, when Mars bought Wrigley's, InBev bought Anheuser-Busch, or when Procter & Gamble bought Gillette – they've tended to pay right around 30 times free cash flow.

So generally speaking, if you can find one of these really great businesses trading for around 15 or 16 times free cash flow, you're probably getting a really good deal that you should buy and hang on to for a long time.

Of course, there's much more to valuing companies than we can explain here, but this will get you started. I also spend a great deal of time explaining these topics to readers of my *Extreme Value* advisory.

S&A: Any parting thoughts?

Ferris: I think there's a temptation for investors just learning to value businesses to focus on the "net worth"-type companies I mentioned earlier – the so-called "deep value" stocks – because they can appear to be much easier to value correctly.

But what you'll come to realize is many of those situations don't work out very well. Oftentimes, what you're really doing is buying a bad business that may be on its last legs.

So after a while, many value investors decide they don't want to buy lousy businesses anymore. They decide they would rather buy great businesses that are going to maintain and grow their value for a long time.

That's a typical transition for a value investor to make, and one I've made myself. In fact, Warren Buffett himself made this transition over his career. I encourage new value investors to keep that in mind.

S&A: That's a great point. Thanks for talking with us.

Ferris: My pleasure. Thanks for inviting me.

Summary: The first step to valuing a stock like a business owner would is to decide you won't buy a stock unless you can understand its business, it looks attractive (i.e. thick profit margins and free cash flow generation), and it's reasonably priced. When you really understand what you're buying, you'll tend to be much more selective and gravitate toward great businesses.

WHAT MAKES FOR A GREAT BUSINESS

This simple idea won't make you a better investor overnight...

But understanding it will give you an advantage most investors will never know. It will put you in the company of legendary investors like Warren Buffett, John Templeton, Marty Whitman, Seth Klarman, and Joel Greenblatt... who have made billions of dollars by relying on it

Any investor who hopes to safely make a fortune in stocks cannot afford to ignore this idea. It's a favorite of Stansberry & Associates' Senior Analyst Dan Ferris. Here's what he has to say...

Stansberry & Associates: Legendary investor Warren Buffett has often said his ideal investment is a wonderful business trading at a fair price. While many investors are familiar with price-to-earnings ratios, price-to-book values, and other measures of value, we hear relatively little about what actually makes a great business. Dan, can you describe what makes a great business?

Dan Ferris: Well, great businesses can be defined a number of ways, but most of them share a few common traits. In my opinion, one of the most important traits is what's known as a durable competitive advantage. Put simply, it's an advantage over the competition that is likely to last for a long time... and often has *already* lasted for a long time.

In capitalism, when a company is extremely successful, you inevitably get competitors coming in. If a company is making an 80% gross margin, someone will come along and say, "I'm going to undercut them and earn a 70% gross margin." Then someone else comes along and says, "I'm perfectly happy with 60%." Before you know it, it's not 80% anymore... it's 8%.

When a company is able to sustain superior performance over a long period of time, it's a clue there's something special going on...

that the company has a tangible advantage in its industry. That's an invaluable trait... and one most of the world's best companies have.

Wal-Mart is so big and efficient, it can do anything any other retailer can do... only much cheaper. ExxonMobil is like that, too. So is UPS. UPS owns an enormous global transportation and logistics network. It's very difficult to compete with. Burlington Northern and other American railroads have an excellent durable competitive advantage. They own thousands of miles of railroad track, and nobody wants anyone to build more railroad track. Once you get a railroad built through a particular area, chances are folks won't want to allow another to be built there. People don't generally like to have railroads and pipelines in their backyards.

S&A: A durable competitive advantage. What's another trait?

Ferris: Another important one is thick profit margins. A thick profit margin generally indicates a business is efficient at allocating capital and controlling costs, so more of its revenue can be retained as profit. It also means the business has a built-in buffer of safety... meaning the risk that a drop in revenue will cause an operating loss is much lower.

Obviously, this means some industries are much more likely to produce great businesses than others... But if a company can maintain a relatively thick, stable profit margin compared to other businesses in the same industry, it's another big sign you're on to a great business.

Thick profit margins are universally desirable. Everybody in business would much rather net $0.20 in profit for every dollar of sales than $0.02. When you're able to hold off competition AND make a thick profit, that's as good a financial result as a business can ever get.

A third characteristic of a great business is low capital expenditures. This basically equates to being able to employ a relatively small amount of capital and get incrementally more growth out of it.

A great example here is Microsoft. Microsoft didn't need to build a factory to produce its new Windows operating system. It didn't need to build a mine or buy a million trucks or a million planes or anything of the sort. It required just a small capital investment, next to none really. It might have needed to hire a few more people. And so it can make a huge return on it. That's a great characteristic.

Warren Buffett often gives the examples of Coca-Cola and See's Candies, because they've required little capital to grow... and they earn so much more now than when he first invested in them.

S&A: Most of the companies you've mentioned are big and super well-known. How important is an elite name brand?

Ferris: A recognizable brand that everybody really wants is a big advantage.

Think about the difference between, say, Hershey and any other candy bar: It's three o'clock in the afternoon, and you feel like having a Hershey bar to get you through the rest of your work day. You walk outside your office and there's a little store on the corner. You go inside, and see some other brand of chocolate bar, but no Hershey. Right across the street, there's a 7-Eleven that you know has Hershey bars. I think many, many people would cross the street for the Hershey bar. THAT is a great brand.

When I shave, I use Gillette. There's just no substitute for it. When I sit down for lunch in a restaurant I've never been to, my first question for the server is, "Coke or Pepsi?" If it's Coke, I'm good. If it's Pepsi, I'll have iced tea. At dinner, my first question is, "Do you have Sam Adams?" I hardly ever drink any other beer. I don't think I'm that unusual. People trust certain brands.

That's one of the reasons McDonald's is so successful. You can get exactly the same food at all 30,000 restaurants. It's uncanny when you think about it, how they're able to make all those identical Big Macs all over the world every day.

I could go on, but you get the picture. They could raise the price of Coke, Big Macs, Sam Adams, or Gillette razors by 10% or even 15%, and it wouldn't faze me a bit. That pricing power is one of the primary attributes that makes an elite brand name so valuable as a business.

Of course, it often goes hand in hand with other traits. Coca-Cola is known all over the world. At the same time, it has the world's largest beverage distribution system... meaning it can sell a lot more of any product than anyone else.

So if you create some new soft-drink product, you can either try to build a distribution system yourself or you can just go to Coke – which has the world's biggest distribution system – and you could conceivably get that product into more people's hands quicker than by any other means.

S&A: Any other traits common among great businesses?

Ferris: There's one more that's also related to the others... and that's scalability. It's not a coincidence that many of the world's greatest businesses become huge blue-chip companies. A great business can be scaled quite easily... So given enough time, many of them grow to be very large.

It's an advantage in some ways. Obviously, it's a hindrance in others. You can't grow as fast once you're big. But you can still grow. And in general, you can pay for that growth much easier than your smaller competitors can.

Like I mentioned before... Wal-Mart is better at cutting costs and moving large amounts of merchandise for a low price than anybody else is. ExxonMobil is better at navigating the cycles of the oil and gas industry than anybody else is.

You can go right down the list and say this company is better at this than anybody else is... and it's how they got so enormously big. Wal-Mart, ExxonMobil, Apple, Microsoft... They are some of the biggest companies in the world, and they're all hugely successful.

That's probably the simplest way to see there's something special going on... that they have something other companies don't.

S&A: Thanks for talking with us, Dan.

Ferris: You're welcome. Take care.

Summary: Great businesses leave clues... Traits like durable competitive advantage, thick profit margins, low capital expenditures, elite name brand, and scalability are predictable signs of the world's greatest companies.

WORLD DOMINATING DIVIDEND GROWERS

For folks interested in safe, reliable investment income, there's one class of stocks that beats all the others.

This class of stocks is the ultimate vehicle for the time-strapped, risk-averse investor. And it can build an incredible amount of wealth over the long term.

To explain this idea, we sat down with Stansberry & Associates' Senior Analyst Dan Ferris.

Stansberry & Associates: Dan, you're a huge proponent of buying a class of dividend-paying stocks you've termed "World Dominating Dividend Growers."

Can you define this idea for us... and tell us why these stocks are such a great idea?

Dan Ferris: I've coined the term "World Dominating Dividend Growers" to describe a small group of elite businesses that dominate their industries. They use their dominant positions to pay their shareholders safe and ever-increasing dividends.

The main thing that separates them from all other stocks is they're the No. 1 company in their industry... the biggest and the best. And they tend to have much better businesses than all their competitors.

A great example of this is Intel. It has got a much better business than AMD – its closest competitor. It's much, much more profitable, and its balance sheet tends to be a lot better. Its products sell a lot more. It dominates 80% of the global semiconductor market... meaning it's four times bigger than the entire rest of the industry.

It has proven its ability to deliver time and time again, more so than any other company in the industry... And consequently, it has had consistently thick profit margins and huge free cash flow generation.

Intel's dividend has also grown consistently since 2004. These are the kind of characteristics you find with a World Dominating Dividend Grower.

Another characteristic of these stocks is they don't just pay a solid dividend... they pay a solid dividend that relentlessly grows every year for years, often several decades.

S&A: What makes them such great places to put money, compared to the average dividend stock?

Ferris: They're great because they're more predictable.

By that, I mean you don't have to worry too much about what a company like Wal-Mart is going to look like in five or even 10 years. You don't wonder what Procter & Gamble will be doing in 10 years. I think they'll both be bigger, and doing almost exactly what they're doing now. That predictability is really, really valuable.

It can often be very difficult to figure out the value of many stocks. The value today is technically worth all the future cash you're going to get out of the business. If you're looking at a mining company, an oil and gas company, or even an insurance company, you don't know what they're going to be charging five or 10 years from now for the product they sell... and it's largely out of their control. They can't just raise prices to keep pace with inflation when their costs rise.

On the other hand, Coca-Cola can raise the price of a soda another nickel or dime and nobody cares. Pricing power is just one aspect of the predictability but it's a significant part of it.

It's also fairly predictable it's going to be in excellent financial condition this year, next year, and five or 10 years from now. It's going to have great balance sheets, and it's generally going to take good care of the money it makes for shareholders.

That predictability translates into less risk. Less risk is really important... much more important than trying to get a higher return.

The fact is, successful investors don't tend to be people who swing for the fences and try to make 50%, 60%, 100% a year. They're people who avoid risk over a long period of time.

S&A: What else makes World Dominators such great stocks to own?

Ferris: These stocks are also one of the greatest compounding vehicles in the world today. And compounding is the surest way to build a great deal of wealth.

The best example of compounding I've ever heard can be illustrated with a simple question: If you start with a penny and double it every day, how long until you have $1 million? Many people will guess several months... I've even heard someone say a year or two. But the answer is just 28 days.

That's an extreme example, obviously no one's going to make 100% per day, but it's a great example. The second day you only go up by one penny, then by four cents, and before you know it you pass a million bucks. That's the way compounding works. In the beginning you don't see it so much, but over time you see it a lot.

Another well-known example is Warren Buffett's position in Coca-Cola. Buffett bought Coke back in 1987, and he's now getting 50% of his purchase price back every year in dividends. He's compounding his money at an enormously high rate. Why would he ever sell an investment like that?

Imagine an investment where you get 50% of your original purchase price back every year. It's an investor's dream. And the surest, safest way to get that is to buy a World Dominating Dividend Grower at a good price and just wait. That's all it takes, but people rarely do it – most people simply don't have the patience.

Over the last 80-plus years, dividends accounted for about 44% of the total return of the S&P 500. As of 2011, reinvesting all dividends produced eight times the return as the S&P 500 without dividends.

S&A: You mentioned buying these stocks at the right price...

How do you determine a great price for a World Dominating Dividend Grower?

Ferris: Almost any stock can be a good investment if you get it cheap enough. But when you can get a World Dominator that has been growing dividends for 50 years cheap enough, that's one of the greatest opportunities in the investment world.

"Cheap enough" for these stocks is pretty easy to figure out. These stocks are all huge cash-gushers. In most circumstances, they have so much cash, you have to assume quite a bit of it is redundant and unnecessary and should be paid out to shareholders. So you want to subtract that cash from the market capitalization. That gives you a price for the actual business.

When it comes to World Dominating Dividend Growers, any time the price for that actual business is under 15 times the company's cash flow, it's really attractive. Sometimes, you can buy them at 12 or 13 times cash flow. It's amazing.

Any time these valuations get down to the low double digits or even single digits – which is absurdly cheap for these companies – you know you've got a fantastic buy.

It doesn't matter that most of these companies will never be taken over by a private company... It matters that it is earning an enormous return on shareholder equity. That's where your return comes from when you hold a stock over time.

S&A: Do you recommend a specific buying strategy or position sizing for these stocks?

Ferris: For any stock you plan to hold as an investment, legging into it over a period of weeks or even a couple months is usually smart. That's my preferred method for World Dominating Dividend Growers.

As far as position sizing – meaning what percentage of your portfolio you put into any one stock – you can safely buy a little more than you might typically. I generally suggest anywhere from

3%-5% of your assets, or even more if you're really confident and really up to speed on a company.

S&A: You've mentioned the ultimate goal with these stocks is to buy them when they're cheap, reinvest the dividends, and compound your wealth by holding for a long period of time. Under what circumstances would you sell them?

Ferris: Well, no company is perfect forever. Most companies lose their competitive advantage over time, or at least weaken and succumb to competition. Maybe bad management will take over.

There are many reasons why a company might eventually stop performing. And when I say performing, I'm talking about the business, not the stock. That's true of World Dominators, like it is for any other stock. It's relatively rare, but they're not immune.

We always assume the stock will eventually reflect the performance of the business. So if that happens, that's when you need to start thinking about selling.

Another time you might consider selling is when a stock gets expensive. When a stock gets expensive, it's delivering years of return upfront. In many cases, it's wise to take it off the table. When the market says, "You don't have to wait, I'm going to pay you now," you should let it do that. That has been a hard lesson for me to learn, but in many cases I think it makes good sense and can greatly increase your returns. And you can always buy the stock back once it returns to a more reasonable valuation, assuming nothing else about the business has changed.

Of course, there's a case to be made for holding as well. Coke was trading at 88 times earnings in 2000 and Buffett never sold. Now he's making 50% a year in dividends. When you buy a great stock at a great price, you can afford to hold through ups and downs.

S&A: Great point. Thanks for talking with us, Dan.

Ferris: My pleasure.

Summary: "World Dominating Dividend Grower" stocks are the No. 1 businesses in their industries. They have thick profit margins, fortress balance sheets, and pay out large and growing dividends to shareholders. Because WDDGs are so good at what they do, and because of their dominant position in their industries, they are extremely resistant to outside competition. This allows their shareholders to safely compound their wealth over many years.

ECONOMIC GOODWILL

This idea is a little different.

It's simple... but often misunderstood. It's not an investment strategy... yet it's the secret behind the success of investment greats like Warren Buffett.

It's about buying great stocks at the right price.

For Stansberry & Associates founder Porter Stansberry's quick and easy-to-understand explanation, read on...

Stansberry & Associates: Economic goodwill is probably one of the least understood ideas in investing. Can you define this idea and explain why it's such an important concept for investors?

Porter Stansberry: Economic goodwill is an accounting term that refers to the intangible assets of a company. It's a simple idea, but a tough subject for most people to get their heads around.

All the excess value of a company – all the stuff that isn't property, equipment, inventory, etc. – goes into the catch-all category of goodwill.

The SEC requires companies to write off goodwill over time. The precise rules around goodwill are beyond the scope of this conversation, but there are various tests done against goodwill that the companies then have to appropriately price.

The effect of this is, over time, companies lose the value of their goodwill according to these accounting standards. But in fact, the goodwill of many businesses actually increases over time.

So the bottom line is that the book value of many companies – especially great companies – is often misstated, because there isn't enough credit given to the goodwill column.

S&A: Can you explain why that is?

Stansberry: Sure... let me give you an example.

If you look at the balance sheet of a company like Coca-Cola, you're going to find a certain amount of value given to goodwill.

But that goodwill – that number on the balance sheet – doesn't compute when you look closely. The company is able to produce enormous returns on net-tangible assets that cannot be explained in the context of free markets. Coke's annual return is something near 90% a year. That doesn't make any sense. That's an unbelievably high return.

It doesn't make any sense because Coke's true net-tangible assets are actually much higher... The true economic goodwill that Coke has is not represented anywhere on its balance sheet.

So the trick to economic goodwill is to understand there is this invisible asset that can play a huge role in corporate earnings. Coke is able to charge more for carbonated sugar water than the oil companies can charge for gasoline. That doesn't make economic sense, unless you understand the value of its brand... the value of the relationship it has with its customers.

It's the same story for companies like Harley-Davidson, Tiffany's, Hershey, etc. These companies that have great relationships with their customers... they have powerful brands... the goodwill that is written out on their balance sheets is totally unrelated to the actual value.

S&A: How can investors take advantage of this fact?

Stansberry: Because of this discrepancy, these companies can appear to be expensive in the context of normal accounting, but may actually be trading at very low prices. This can be a huge advantage if you know what to look for.

As another example, I recommended Hershey in my newsletter a few years ago. At the time, Hershey only had about $500 million of goodwill on its balance sheet.

In comparison, Hershey's total assets were close to $4 billion. It had about $2 billion in current assets, which basically means cash. But what's more important to realize is it only had $250 million of net-tangible assets. It's hard to believe, but it's true, because it also had close to $3.5 billion in debt.

Now, that's not necessarily a bad thing. When you have a stable business like Hershey, it can make good sense to finance your operations with borrowed money.

But the important point is Hershey's net-tangible assets were stated at just $250 million... yet the company makes a billion dollars in cash per year.

This means Hershey's return on net-tangible assets was 400%. That is out of this world... completely off the charts. Has Hershey discovered some secret to earning bigger returns than any company in history, or is something else going on? Of course, the answer is goodwill... It's dramatically undervalued on the balance sheet.

In other words, the most valuable thing it owned was only stated as $500 million, or about 12.5% of its total assets. There's no way Hershey's goodwill was that small.

The truth is, goodwill is worth more than all of its other assets combined. It's difficult to price exactly what that goodwill is worth, but we think it's high because the company makes so much money every year.

We can estimate it by thinking about what a reasonable return on net-tangible assets might be. In this case, let's suppose Hershey's true return on net-tangible assets was about 10%. That's a solid return for a company like Hershey.

To get that return, net-tangible assets would actually have been $10 billion rather than the $250 million stated on the balance sheet. This means the company would actually have about $6 billion in "invisible assets" – $10 billion in total assets versus the $4 billion stated on the balance sheet – that didn't show up on the balance sheet. This means goodwill was probably closer to $6 billion than the $500 million we talked about earlier... so it was actually about 10 times higher than stated.

Of course, that's just a simplified example. The point is that companies' balance sheets are often times undervalued relative to the real economic value of their goodwill.

In this example, Hershey's true return on net-tangible assets could be higher or lower, but it's clear that Hershey's goodwill is undervalued on its balance sheet. Because of that, some measures of value will indicate Hershey is more expensive than it actually is.

S&A: Are there any other clues that a company has much more goodwill than its balance sheet suggests?

Stansberry: Most companies that have a lot of economic goodwill are heavily branded companies. They're companies with a long history of a consumer love affair, which is probably the best way to describe it.

A great example I mentioned earlier is Harley-Davidson. People who buy Harley-Davidson motorcycles tend to be fanatics. The economic goodwill in that company is generated by the loyalty and the dedication of its customers, and that is really what fuels the returns.

There are companies that aren't strongly branded that have economic goodwill, but they're few and far between.

But again, the best way to uncover these discrepancies in goodwill is to look at the net-tangible assets of a company relative to its cash earnings.

S&A: Does economic goodwill have any other benefits?

Stansberry: The other great thing about goodwill is that it doesn't require much capital to maintain.

Let's go back to the Hershey example and assume the true value of its goodwill was closer to $6 billion than $500 million.

Well, if it had another $6 billion worth of traditional assets on its balance sheet, it would have to invest a lot of capital to maintain those assets, right? If there are billions more in property, equipment, and inventory, it would require a significant amount of capital to maintain and replenish those assets.

If it had another $5 billion in assets, it might have to spend another billion dollars per year just to maintain it. But if it did that, of course, it wouldn't have any earnings at all because it was only earning a billion dollars in cash.

So the real value of economic goodwill is that it doesn't cost much to maintain. It's a huge value that is unseen on your balance sheet and doesn't cost you any money to maintain.

This is really, really powerful, especially in the context of inflation, because over time, Hershey will be able to raise the price of its chocolate bars in line with inflation. You've seen this happen again and again your entire life.

A Hershey bar used to cost $0.05, then it was $0.10, then it was $0.25, and so on. Well, now it's $1.50. But throughout all that time, Hershey hasn't had to spend any more money maintaining its economic goodwill.

It has had to spend more money on materials to make chocolate. It has had to spend more money on shipping and energy. But it hasn't had to spend a penny extra to maintain its economic goodwill. That is why economic goodwill tends to compound at a very high rate over time.

In another 30 years, Hershey's economic goodwill might be $60 billion instead of $6 billion. And Hershey wouldn't have had to spend any capital to maintain it.

That's a very valuable thing for a company. Instead of having to spend money maintaining that economic goodwill, it can spend it on dividends to shareholders.

That's the real secret behind Warren Buffett's success. He has specialized in investing over the long term in economic goodwill, and the result speaks for itself.

S&A: That's a great explanation, Porter. Thanks for talking with us.

Stansberry: You're welcome.

Summary: Businesses with lots of economic goodwill have strong consumer franchises. (Folks think of "Coke" when they hear soda and they think "Hershey" when they hear chocolate.) This brand loyalty allows them to generate high returns on capital with little additional ongoing investment. They can raise prices as needed. Higher prices translate into more money returned to shareholders... for years and years.

THE EASIEST WAY TO MAKE $1 MILLION IN THE STOCK MARKET

Of all the investment ideas out there, the idea of compounding is king.

It is by far the most powerful investment idea in the world. It's the ultimate way for investors to safely and surely build long-term wealth in the stock market. Albert Einstein even famously said that compounding is "the greatest mathematical discovery of all time."

In the interview that follows, *Retirement Millionaire* editor Dr. David Eifrig explains the power of this idea. "Doc," as many people call him, is an expert at finding low-risk, high-reward investment opportunities.

Read on to discover how you can put this simple, yet extremely powerful strategy to work...

Stansberry & Associates: Doc, you've called compounding the "easiest way to make $1 million in the stock market," and "the No. 1 strategy for retiring wealthy."

Can you tell us what it is and how it works?

Dr. David Eifrig: Sure... But before I go on, let me warn you. Compounding is not a get-rich-quick idea. It's not about making 100% overnight. It's about safely building wealth over the long term.

It starts with one simple idea... compound returns.

Simply stated, compound returns are money you make off the money you make. And the more money you make, the more money your money makes off the money your money makes. Here's how it happens...

Imagine you're 40 years old, have a $10,000 investment account, and subscribe to my *Retirement Millionaire* letter. In one year, our portfolio's conservative blend of assets returned a fantastic 18%.

If you kept reading year after year and kept making consistent 18% annual returns, what would happen to your portfolio by the time you retire at the age of 68?

You'd have earned a million dollars.

S&A: That sounds almost too good to be true. Can you break the numbers down for us?

Eifrig: The numbers are simple: If you start investing with $10,000 at the end of the first year, you'll have about $11,800 (not including taxes or fees). You made $1,800 on your initial investment.

But in your second year... you're not starting over at $10,000. The $1,800 you earned in the first year will be making money for you, too.

So assuming gains of 18%, you'll have earned another $1,800 on your original capital plus another $324 on the profits from the previous year's $1,800.

You're not just multiplying $1,800 times 25 years. (That only gives you $45,000.) Where does the other $903,000 come from? That's the secret.

The money starts making money on top of itself – your money is compounding.

The money you make in the first year, in this case $1,800, starts making money in the second year, third year, and so on... It continues this way for every stream of money you compound. So the $1,800 you make in your second year also makes $324 in the third.

But there's more. The $324 you make in the second year generated by your first $1,800 now makes $58.32 on itself in the third year. Take a look at the diagram below and you'll see how by the end of your third year, you'll have $16,430.

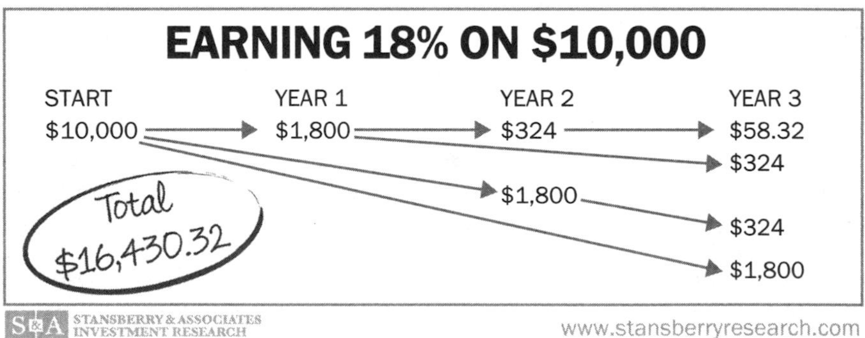

And the money just keeps building. Take a look at the chart below. You can see how much money you'll have at the end of each year.

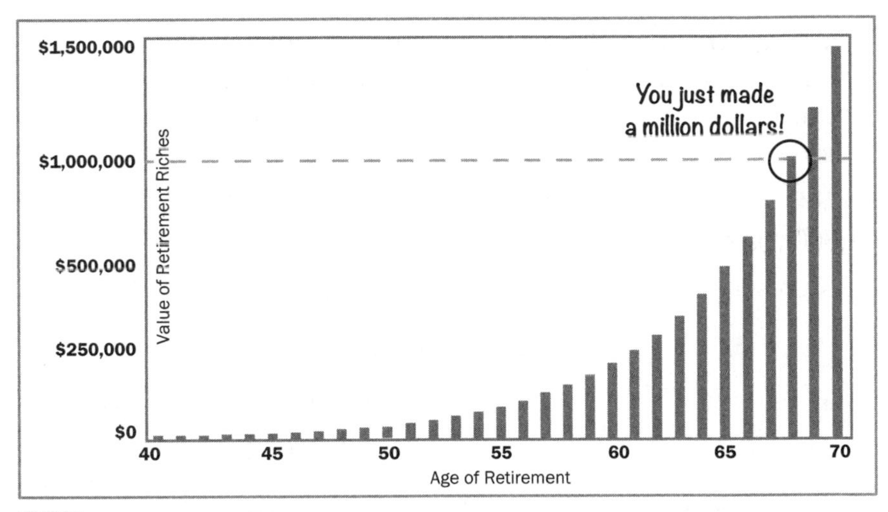

By age 68 (28 years of compounding), it totals nearly $1 million. And if you wait another couple years, until age 70, the compounding effect starts to explode. At that point, you have almost $1.5 million.

You can see why this secret is so powerful. By plowing your earnings back into your portfolio, you can get your money working for itself and amass a fortune from your initial investments.

It sounds almost nonsensical... but if you start with a $10,000 portfolio at age 40, you can have more than $1 million by the time you retire.

And as it turns out, that's chump change.

S&A: Chump change? Please explain...

Eifrig: I'll show you what I mean with the story of my father and my sister.

Both of them used the power of compounding to create a worry-free retirement. But the results were vastly different.

With his retirement account, my dad took advantage of the power of compounding.

My sister did, too. She lives in Bozeman, Montana with her husband and two sons. Their house offers a beautiful view of the mountains. They have the time and money to do most anything they want. I shared the secret of compounding with her about 25 years ago... and she credits me with showing her the way to become a millionaire.

You can see compounding action in this chart:

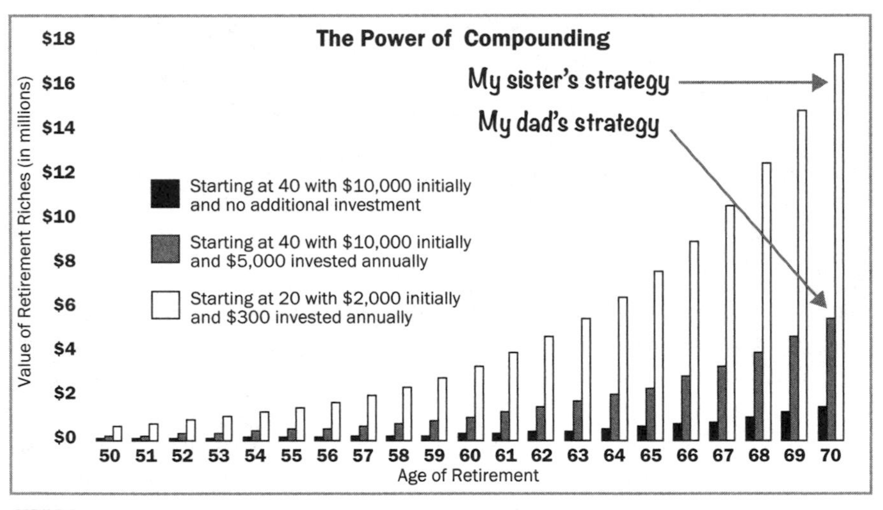

The black bars represent the strategy I showed you first... And it works: $10,000 turns into more than $1 million.

But look at the other bars...

The gray bars represent my dad's strategy. In my father's case, he started tucking a little bit of money away each year in the retirement plan his university offered for professors. I don't have the exact numbers. But it wasn't as much as the initial amount he used to open the account.

You can see how starting with $10,000 and then just putting $5,000 a year for the next 20 years makes a person a millionaire by age 60. That's nearly eight years sooner than the plan I showed you previously.

If you continue for just another five years – 25 years total – you're a multimillionaire. If you maintain this strategy until age 68, you'll be worth nearly $4 million... $3.862 million to be exact.

Think about this for a minute. You start at age 40, earning what we've been earning in my *Retirement Millionaire* newsletter (18%) in a balanced and safe mix of securities. You begin with $10,000 and add a little bit more each year ($5,000). And voilá... You're a millionaire at age 60.

Now look at the white bars, which represent my sister's strategy.

What my sister did was apply these same principles in her first job. And she made sure that for every job and raise thereafter, she added a little bit more to the retirement kitty.

But for her, it was much easier. She started a lot younger and didn't have to put much in (she didn't have much to put in). The chart shows what happens if, like my sister, you start at age 20 with only $2,000 and put in just $300 a year after that... You become a millionaire by age 54.

At that point, you've put in a total of $10,200 – and earned $990,000 on the original investments. And if you wait five more years, you become a multimillionaire at age 59. That's a spectacular return on an $11,700 investment plan. It's 17,000% if you're scoring at home.

The key for my sister was that she started early. She used the power of time to build a lot of wealth.

S&A: Wow. Those are some incredible numbers, Doc. Are there any final thoughts you want to share?

Eifrig: Well, as I showed you with my father's story, you don't need 50 years to appreciate the power of compounding. But as my sister's example proves, the more time you have, the more you can supercharge the power of compounding.

So I suggest you share this "secret" with your friends and family. If you have children or grandchildren, they need to know about saving and investing. One way to teach them is with the story of my sister... how she started with a small amount, added some money every year, and saw it grow to millions of dollars. And it was all due to the power of compounding.

S&A: Thanks for talking with us, Doc.

Eifrig: You're welcome.

Summary: Compounding is the process of taking the earnings, dividends, or interest that you make from an investment... and then buying more of the investment. Over time, it allows your money to accumulate into a big snowball of money.

The trick to building significant wealth with compounding is all about patience and time. The earlier you start, the better off you are. This is why compounding is such a key idea to teach young people.

PERSONAL FINANCE

ASSET ALLOCATION

The most important factor in your investment success isn't about picking "hot" stocks... and it's not about finding the next great country to invest in.

The most important factor in your investment success is **100 times more important than any stock pick**.

It's 100 times more important than what the housing market is doing... or whether the economy is booming or busting.

Not taking this idea into account has ruined more retirements than any other financial factor...

We're talking about asset allocation.

As a former professional trader at one of the world's top investment banks, no one is more qualified to speak about this idea than Dr. David "Doc" Eifrig.

What you'll find below is not complicated, but it could be the most important investment idea you ever learn...

Stansberry & Associates: Doc... many investors spend a lot of time and energy trying to pick the right stocks. But one's success as a stock picker actually plays a relatively small role when it comes to increasing wealth through investment... much smaller than the average investor realizes.

A much more important aspect to successful investment is called asset allocation. Can you explain what this is, and why it's so important?

Dr. David Eifrig: I'd be happy to. Asset allocation is how you balance your wealth among stocks, bonds, cash, real estate, commodities, and precious metals in your portfolio. This mix is the most important factor in your retirement investing success.

It's 100 times more important than any stock pick. It's 100 times more important than knowing the next hot country to invest in... or what option to buy... or knowing what the housing market is doing... or whether the economy is booming or busting.

I've seen ignorance of this topic ruin more retirements than any other financial factor.

S&A: How can it ruin a retirement?

Eifrig: Many people have no idea what sensible asset allocation is... So they end up taking huge risks by sticking big chunks of their portfolios into just one or two investments.

For example, I have a friend who had most of her wealth in real estate investments in 2006. When the market busted, she lost a huge portion of her retirement funds.

Or consider employees of big companies that put a huge portion of their retirement money into company stock. Employees of big companies that went bankrupt, like Enron, WorldCom, Bear Stearns, and Lehman Brothers were totally wiped out. They believed in the companies they worked for, so they kept more than half of their retirement portfolios into company stock.

And it's all because they didn't know about proper asset allocation. Because of this ignorance, they lost everything.

I'm sure you can see from these examples that asset allocation is so important because keeping your wealth stored in a good, diversified mix of assets is the key to avoiding catastrophic losses.

If you keep too much wealth – like 80% of it – in a handful of stocks and the stock market goes south, you'll suffer badly. The same goes for any asset... gold, oil, bonds, real estate, or blue-chip stocks. Concentrating your retirement nest egg in just a few different asset classes is way too risky for you. Betting on just one horse is a fool's game.

S&A: This seems like simple common sense... to spread your risk around.

Eifrig: I agree. But not doing it is an extremely common mistake people make.

S&A: Could you walk us through what asset classes are out there... and what a sensible mix looks like?

Eifrig: First off, you have one of my favorite assets in the world, which is cash.

"Cash" simply means all the money you have in savings, checking accounts, certificates of deposit (CDs), and U.S. Treasury bills. Anything with less than one year to maturity should be considered cash.

I like to keep plenty of cash on hand so I can be ready to buy bargains in case of a market collapse. Investors flush with cash are often able to get assets on the cheap after a collapse – they can swoop in and pick things up with cash quickly, and often at great prices.

I generally recommend holding between 10% and 45% of your assets in cash, depending on your circumstances. In fact, one of the major tenets of good financial planning is to always have at least 12 months of living expenses in cash in case of disaster. If you haven't started saving yet, this is the No. 1 thing to start today.

Next, you have conventional stocks. These are investments in individual businesses, or investments in broad baskets of stocks, like mutual funds and exchange-traded funds (ETFs). Stocks are a proven long-term builder of wealth, so I think almost everyone should own some. But keep in mind, stocks are typically more volatile than most other assets.

Just like you should stay diversified overall with your assets, I think you should stay diversified in your stock portfolio. I once heard a well-known TV money show host ask callers: "Are you diversified?" According to him, owning five stocks in different sectors makes you diversified. This is simply not true. It is a dangerous notion.

The famous economist Harry Markowitz modeled math, physics, and stock-picking to win a Nobel Prize for the work on diversification. The science showed you need around 12-18 stocks to be fully diversified.

Holding and following that many stocks might seem daunting – it's really not. The problem is easily solved with a mutual fund that holds dozens of stocks, which of course makes you officially diversified.

S&A: Let's discuss a few more asset categories.

Eifrig: Next, you have fixed-income securities, with are generally called "notes" or "bonds." These are basically any instrument that pays out a regular stream of income over a fixed period of time. At the end, you also get your initial investment – which is called your "principal" – back.

Depending on your age and tolerance for risk, bonds sit somewhere between boring and a godsend. The promise of interest payments and an almost certain return of capital at a certain fixed rate for a long period of time always lets me sleep well at night.

Adding safe fixed-income bonds to your portfolio is a simple way to stabilize your investment returns over time. For people with enough capital, locking up extra money (more than 12 months of your expenses) in bonds is a simple way to generate more income than a savings account.

Another asset class is real estate. Everyone knows what this is, so we don't need to spend much time covering this. If you can keep a portion of wealth in a paid-for home, and possibly some income-producing real estate like a rental property or a farm, it's a great diversifier.

S&A: Do you consider precious metals, like gold and silver, an important piece of a sensible asset allocation?

Eifrig: I do... But gold and silver, to me, are like insurance.

Precious metals like gold and silver typically soar during times of economic turmoil, so I want to own some "just in case."

But I'm different than the standard owner of gold and silver, who almost always believes the world is headed for hell in a hand basket.

I'm a major optimist, but I'm also a realist. I believe in owning insurance. I believe in staying "hedged."

For many years, my job at Wall Street bank Goldman Sachs was to develop and implement advanced hedging strategies for wealthy clients and corporations. The goal with these strategies was to protect jobs, wealth, and profits from unforeseen events.

During those years, I learned a big difference between wealthy people and poor people. Wealthy people almost always own plenty of hedges and insurance. They consider what could happen in worst-case scenarios and take steps to protect themselves. Poor people tend to live with "blinders" on.

So just like I wear my seat belt while driving, I own silver and gold – just in case. For most people, most of the time, keeping around 5% of your wealth in gold and silver provides that insurance.

S&A: That's a great view of gold and silver. So... you've covered five broad categories... cash, stocks, bonds, real estate, and precious metals. Do you have any guidelines on how much of each asset folks should own?

Eifrig: There's no way anyone can provide a "one size fits all" allocation. Everyone's financial situation is different. Asset allocation advice that will work for one person can be worthless for another.

But most of us have the same basic goals: Wealth preservation... picking up safe income... and safely growing our nest egg. We can all use some guidelines to help make the right individual choices. Keep in mind, what I'm about to say are just guidelines...

If you're having a hard time finding great bargains in stocks and bonds, I think an allocation of 25%... even 50% in cash is a good idea.

This sounds crazy to some people, but if you can't find great investment bargains, there's nothing wrong with sitting in cash, earning a little interest, and being patient. If great bargains present themselves, like they did in early 2009, you can lower your cash balance and plow it into stocks and bonds.

As for stocks, if you're younger and more comfortable with the volatility involved in stocks, you can keep a stock exposure to somewhere around 33%-50% of your portfolio. A young person who can place a sizable chunk of money into a group of high-quality, dividend-paying stocks and hold them for decades will grow very wealthy.

If you're older and can't stand risk or volatility, consider keeping a huge chunk of your wealth in cash and bonds... like a 75%-85% weighting. Near the end of your career as an investor, you're more concerned with preserving wealth than growing it, so you want to be very conservative.

S&A: Great advice. Any last thoughts?

Eifrig: As you can see from my guidelines, the big thing to keep in mind with asset allocation is that you've got to find a mix that is right for you... that suits your risk tolerance... your station in life.

Whatever mix you choose, just make sure you're not overexposed to an unforeseen crash in one particular asset. This will ensure a long and profitable investment career.

S&A: Thanks, Doc.

Elfrig: You're welcome.

Summary: Asset allocation is how you balance your wealth among stocks, bonds, cash, real estate, commodities, and precious metals in your portfolio. It is the single most important factor in your success as an investor.

WHY I'LL NEVER RETIRE

Over the last 30 years, Mark Ford has built a reputation as one of the country's foremost experts on wealth building. But unlike most "experts" in this field, Mark actually walks the walk.

He's a serial entrepreneur and *New York Times* bestselling author who has built hundreds of businesses... and a huge personal fortune. A born teacher, Mark now spends his time with family, mentoring entrepreneurs, and managing his investments. He also shares his unconventional wealth ideas to hundreds of thousands of people in his books and financial newsletters.

For our money, no one in America delivers straight, no B.S. financial advice as well as Mark Ford. For his unique view on conventional retirement, read on...

Stansberry & Associates: Mark, you're super-rich...

Mark Ford: Let's just say that I am rich enough to know something about wealth.

S&A: Fine. I've also heard that you've retired several times... and you've developed some ideas on retirement that a lot of people would call radical.

Ford: I joke that I am an expert on retirement because I tried it three times. I was never truly successful.

S&A: How so?

Ford: I discovered that the conventional dream of retirement – however wonderful as an imagined goal – was not very satisfying as a reality. I retired first when I was 39 and went back into the working world about 18 months later. I retired again when I was 50 – and went back with an improved idea about retirement but that wasn't perfect, either. When I was 60, I "retired" for the third time. I think I've got most of the bugs worked out.

S&A: What sort of bugs?

Ford: Well the biggest bug is the mistake I discovered the first time I retired. I had a net worth of about $10 million at the time. I thought that was more than enough to live the rest of my years in luxurious comfort.

S&A: what happened?

Ford: For one thing, $10 million in muni bonds at the time was giving me a return of about $600,000. And even though that was tax-free, my spending habits had already exceeded that. (My *lifestyle burn rate*, as I like to call it, was about $700,000 at the time.) I discovered I couldn't live off the interest on that very substantial asset base.

S&A: What did you do?

Ford: First, I tried to live on a budget. I called in my personal assistant and had her prepare a list of all my living expenses. Then I went through them with her one by one, trying to cut my expenses in half.

S&A: And?

Ford: I couldn't do it. I had to face the fact that in creating wealth I had turned myself into a wealth-consuming addict.

S&A: So what did you do then?

Ford: I went back to work. I took a job as a consultant.

S&A: What did that teach you?

Ford: That the biggest mistake retired people make is giving up all their active income.

S&A: What do you mean by "active income"?

Ford: When I say active income, I mean the money you make through your labor or through a business you own.

Passive income refers to the income you get from Social Security, a pension, or from a retirement account. You can increase your active income by working more. But the only way you can increase your passive income is by getting higher rates of return on your investment.

S&A: Why is giving up an active income so harmful?

Ford: When you give up your active income, two bad things happen:

First, your connection to your active income is cut off. With every month that passes, it becomes more difficult to get it back.

Second, your ability to make smart investment decisions drops because of your dependence on passive income.

Retirement is a wonderful idea: put a portion of your income into an investment account for 40 years and then withdraw from it for the rest of your life. Once you retire, you won't have to work anymore. Instead, you will fill your days with fun activities: traveling, golfing, going to the movies, and visiting the kids and grandkids.

But consider this: A relatively modest retirement lifestyle for two, like the one I described above, would cost about $75,000 a year, or $100,000 before taxes.

How big of a retirement account do you need to fund that?

S&A: Well, if your retirement account were in mutual funds...

Ford: You'd need about $2 million.

S&A: That's a lot more than most folks have saved.

Ford: Exactly.

S&A: What about Social Security and pension plans?

Ford: Putting aside the very real question of whether such institutions are viable and would pay out as promised when you retire, let's assume that you and your spouse could count on $25,000 a year from Social Security and another $25,000 from a pension plan (two big "ifs"). Now say that savings accounts only pay 1%. To earn the $50,000 balance in the safest way possible (from a savings account), you'd need about $5 million.

If you were willing to take a bit more risk and invest in tax-free municipal bonds (this is the safety level I like), you'd need about $1.25 million, assuming you could get 4% interest.

But middle-class American couples my age are trying to retire with an account in the $250,000 to $300,000 range. And that's where the trouble begins. To achieve an annual return of $50,000 on $300,000, you'd need to make 17% a year.

Getting 17% consistently over, say, 20 years may not be impossible, but it's very risky – too risky for my tastes.

And that's why I so strongly recommend that everyone should maintain an active income.

As I said before, when I retired for the first time at 39, I realized not only that I was a spending addict but that to make the kind of returns I needed I had to take more financial risk. I didn't want to take more financial risk because I knew it would make me sleep poorly. Golfing in the daytime and worrying about money at night is not my idea of an ideal retirement.

S&A: So you got a job as a consultant.

Ford: Yes. I went back to a business that I understood from previous experience – I was able to reconnect with colleagues, relearn old skills, and start earning active income again.

S&A: But is that feasible for everyone?

Ford: At some level, yes. Take my brother in law, for example. He's a plumber. He retired and went back to work as a plumbing inspector. That gave him a steady income again.

S&A: So after retiring three times, what's your advice to our readers?

Ford: Don't give up that second income. You can ratchet back, take on less work, switch jobs, go part-time, whatever. But don't give it up entirely.

S&A: And for those that have already done so?

Ford: Get back into it. Everyone has valuable skills. There is always an opportunity if you are willing to work hard to find it.

S&A: How did it feel to go back to work? Was it depressing?

Ford: Not at all. In fact, the moment I started earning money again, I started to feel better.

S&A: That's interesting.

Ford: Retirement isn't supposed to be filled with money worries. And yet, that is exactly what you will get if you try to get above-par returns on your investments.

Millions of Americans my age are quitting their jobs and selling their businesses. They are reading financial magazines and subscribing to newsletters. They are hoping to find a stock-selection system that will give them the 30% and 40% returns they need.

But they will soon find out that such systems don't exist. They will have good months and bad years, and they will compensate for those bad years by taking on more risk. The situation will go from bad to worse.

S&A: Sounds ominous.

Ford: But it doesn't have to be that way.

Let's go back to the example of the couple with the $300,000 retirement fund and the $100,000-a-year retirement dream. To generate the $50,000 they need, they would have to earn about 17% a year in stocks. As I said, that is highly improbable. But if they each earned only $15,000 in active income, they would need a return of only about 7% on their retirement account, which is doable.

There are many ways for a retired person to earn a part-time, active income. You could do some consulting, start your own Web business, or earn money doing any sort of purposeful work.

I am not saying that you should give up on the idea of retirement.

On the contrary, I'm saying that retirement might be more possible than you think.

S&A: But you have to give up conventional retirement thinking, right?

Ford: Yes... you must replace the old, defective idea that retirement means living off passive income only.

Paint a new mental picture of what retirement can be: a life free from financial worry that includes lots of travel, fun, and leisure, funded in part by active income from doing some sort of meaningful work.

The first benefit of including an active income in your retirement planning is that you will be able to generate more money when you need to. But the other benefit – the one that no one talks about – is that it will allow you to make wiser investment decisions because you won't be a slave to your investments.

S&A: That's an interesting – and useful – way to view retirement. Thanks, Mark.

Ford: You're welcome.

Summary: Instead of retiring and giving up all of your "active" income... and then taking big risks to increase your nest egg, consider Mark's unconventional "never retire" idea. By maintaining an active income, you'll be a wiser investor.

THE "THREE-BUCKET SYSTEM" FOR MANAGING MONEY

Mark Ford is one of the smartest people we know when it comes to money. He's always brilliant at finding unorthodox ways to make a buck.

In this interview, Mark describes the money-management system he's used to generate more than $50 million in wealth. Mark's system is simple. But based on his experience, that's the key to a successful wealth-building strategy...

Stansberry & Associates: Mark, you come from humble beginnings... the son of a teacher... one of many children... and today, you're one of the wealthiest men in the country. You've used a unique money-management system to build your fortune. Could you explain your "three-bucket system"?

Mark Ford: Yes. I separate my money into three "buckets": one for spending, one for saving, and one for investing.

I call it the "three-bucket system." It's one of the most important lessons I ever learned about managing money.

When I first started making a bit of money back in 1983, Sid, my surrogate Jewish uncle and my personal accountant, invited me to lunch to talk about the "facts of life."

Sid's intention, I was relieved to discover, was not to cue me in on the birds and bees (I was 33 at the time), but to tell me how to manage my money.

"There are basically three things you can do with money," he said. "You can spend it. You can save it. You can invest it."

Having grown up poor, I was more than excited about spending my money. Sid had noticed that, by observing my checkbook activity.

"Mark," he said. "You're a *mensch*. But when it comes to money, you're acting like a *schlemiel*. How will you ever get rich if you keep spending as much as you make?" he asked me.

"But I'm buying things that have value," I protested. I offered two new cars and some jewelry for my wife as examples.

"Don't be a *schmuck*," he exhorted. "Those are depreciating assets... You might as well put your cash in a blender."

I knew he was right. So I promised him I would begin to "save" money.

"That's not enough!" he snorted. "Saving doesn't do *bupkis* but pay future expenses. You can't get rich by paying future bills. You have to invest to grow wealthy."

I had no idea what he was talking about. At that time, being new to money, I never considered that there could be a difference between saving and investing.

I admitted I was confused. I asked for clarification.

S&A: So what did Sid tell you?

Ford: He told me that the purpose of saving is to take care of *short-term* expenses and avoid *debt*.

To take care of *future* expenses, you want to put your cash in a safe place that earns above market returns. The purpose of investing is to *increase* wealth over the longer term.

S&A: This seems like common sense...

Ford: Another way to look at it is to think of the three buckets in terms of time.

The spending bucket is what you will spend in the next six months to two years. The idea is to always have that amount of money available before you need it. Some financial planners call this an emergency fund, but I prefer thinking of it as spending money, because the way life works, it almost certainly will be spent.

The savings bucket is for a medium-term time frame: three to 10 years. This is the money you will need to pay for a down payment on your house or rental real estate or a car. (I don't believe in leasing cars since they are depreciating assets.)

Finally, the longer-term investment bucket is for the long haul: 10 to 50 or 60 years, depending on how old you are. This is the account that will make you wealthy. The more you can put into this account every month, the better.

Your eventual wealth is based on three things: how much you put into your investment bucket, how long you have it there, and how much risk you take with it. You must position your investment bucket for maximum growth over a defined period of time. The longer the time perspective, the better.

S&A: So how do these buckets differ in terms of what you put in them?

Ford: That is a good question. You want to fill the spending bucket with cash and cash-based instruments like CDs and money-market funds. Vehicles that are very safe and very liquid. Things that won't go down in value.

In the savings bucket, you put financial instruments that, on average, will give you a good market return over a three- to 10-year period. That might include stocks and bonds and real estate.

The key here is you should feel relatively comfortable that when you need to use this money for college or retirement, for example, your investments will be worth at least as much as they were originally, *including inflation*. The primary goal is to protect and preserve real value, not to grow it.

S&A: And the investment bucket?

Ford: You want investments designed specifically for the long term, like high-quality, dividend-paying stocks, bonds, and other investments that allow long-term compounding to occur. These are the types of investments that long-term investors like Warren Buffett might own.

S&A: After adopting the three-bucket system to manage your own money, can you share any insights you have gained?

Ford: Among other insights, I learned several things at a gut level.

First of all, spending makes you poorer. Again, this sounds like common sense, but again, most investors commonly ignore it. You have to really ask yourself every time you make a financial decision: "Is this going to make me richer or poorer?"

You may want to rationalize the decision to buy an expensive car by telling yourself that it will "hold its value." But it won't. It will depreciate.

Another big secret is the idea that you should make sure you grow richer every day. This may sound crazy, but it's something I told myself I would do soon after I met Sid. It changed my entire attitude about work, investing, and spending.

S&A: How so?

Ford: Well, for one thing, it made me understand that I could never get rich by investing in stocks alone. Stocks are good investments if you buy the right ones, but they go up and down, as do many financial investments, including gold, by the way. That's why I don't rely on my investments to make me wealthier. I rely on my income.

Since making this decision, I've made it a point to increase my income constantly – even if that meant taking on two or three jobs. And then I put all of that extra income into my long-term investing bucket. It is that single idea, I believe, that accounted for the wealth I acquired.

S&A: We understand that wealth is considerable...

Ford: Let's just say that my great-grandchildren have nothing to worry about.

S&A: That's an interesting – and useful – way to view money management. Thanks, Mark.

Ford: You're welcome.

Summary: The "three-bucket system" is a strategy that involves understanding the difference between spending, saving, and investing. Your spending account should be very liquid. Your savings account should be in assets that will protect and preserve your money. And your investment account should be full of high-quality investments that will allow you to compound your wealth over time.

HOW TO GET A RAISE AT WORK

A self-made millionaire, Mark Ford knows all the tricks in the book for getting rich.

Mark says that earning just a few percentage points more each year will help you become a millionaire by the time you retire.

Your path to wealth must start somewhere. For many people, the path to long-term wealth starts in the workplace...

Stansberry & Associates: Mark, you're a successful entrepreneur... a highly paid consultant... and accomplished writer. You've also built a reputation as one of the country's foremost experts on wealth building.

For many people, the biggest source of potential wealth is their salary.

You've said that earning just a few percentage points more each year will help you become a millionaire by the time you retire.

Could you explain how to get a raise... and how it can make a huge difference to a person's long-term wealth?

Mark Ford: Absolutely... There's no question about it. Earning just a few percentage points more each year can make you much, much richer over a lifetime.

To show you how, let me start with an example...

My brother hired SP for $20,000. On the same day, he hired LJ for $30,000. Keep in mind... I'm using initials to avoid embarrassing these people. They both had the same qualifications: college degrees, a bit of experience interning for investment companies, and the desire to make a lot of money.

SP stood out from day one. He was the first one to work every morning and stayed after everyone else, including my brother, went home at night. LJ was good but rather ordinary.

Flash-forward 13 years. SP is making more than $2 million every year and LJ is making $38,000.

SP has already outpaced LJ by more than $10 million. By the time they both retire, SP will have a net worth well in excess of $50 million, while LJ will be lucky if he has anything in his bank account.

S&A: What accounted for the difference?

Ford: It was not intelligence. It was simply the fact that SP decided to become a superstar while LJ was content to be ordinary.

That's how I see it. But let me try to prove it to you with some simple arithmetic.

Joe Ordinary is 25 years old, makes an ordinary $30,000 per year income, and gets ordinary 3.5% yearly increases. Over a 40-year career, he will make a little more than $2.6 million.

Sarah Superstar, also 25, averages 5% yearly increases. Over the same 40-year period, she will earn $3.8 million – more than $1 million more than Joe.

If Sarah can keep her expenditures down and live on the same amount of money that Joe is making, she will retire a millionaire while Joe will be forced to live on food stamps and handouts.

That's how big a difference a mere 1.5 percentage points can make when we're talking about raises.

And that 1.5% difference, from the studies I've read, is what Sarah can expect by working hard and making smart decisions throughout her career.

S&A: Is there a plan someone can follow to achieve that "extra" 1.5%?

Ford: There is... and if you stick with it, you could become a multimillionaire in no more than 20 years. But there's something even more exciting than that. Your path to wealth must start somewhere. So in addition to that "blueprint," I can also give you a plan to get an increase of at least 10% one year from now...

S&A: To most people, that sounds almost too good to be true. Where do we begin?

Ford: Let's start by taking a look at how salaries work in a typical business environment.

Businesses exist to provide products and services to consumers. Healthy businesses measure their success in terms of their long-term profits.

As an employee of a business, it's your job to help your company produce those long-term profits. You may think your job is something other than that. You may think, for example, that your job is to answer the phone or deliver the mail or write marketing copy. Nothing could be further from the truth. Your job is to produce long-term profits.

The secret to getting above-average raises each year is to accept that as your fundamental responsibility – and to transform the work you are doing now in such a way that it will produce those long-term profits. The better you can do it, the more money you will make. It's as simple as that.

Salespeople generally make more than accountants, right?

That's not because salespeople are smarter than accountants. Nor do they necessarily work harder. But the job they do is seen as more financially valuable than the job accountants do. That is the one and only reason they get paid more.

S&A: What if you are working as a low-ranking employee right now?

Ford: I would tell you not to worry. My plan works just as well for a low-ranking employee as it does for top brass. In fact, it works better.

Conventional business roles and conventional salaries are the reality for 80% of the workforce – for people who come to work and put in a full day and have a good attitude and hope for the best.

For most of the other 20% – people who are smart and willing to work harder – the business world will reward them with better raises and more in total earnings over a 40-year period.

But there is a smaller group of employees – maybe 25% of that 20% (or 4% of the whole) – who will average even higher raises. Those employees will also earn far more throughout their business careers... enough to make it possible for them to retire rich.

There are more than a dozen employees I've worked with personally during the past 20 years who have taken this less-travelled road. None of them are older than 45 (most are in their 30s), and they are already all multimillionaires.

If they continue as they have been – and there is no reason why they shouldn't – they will all be among the top one-half of 1% of the population in wealth when they decide to retire.

S&A: So let's talk about how someone can make that happen for himself.

Ford: Start with this: Make a commitment to become the most valuable employee in your department in six months and the most valuable employee in your boss' view in one year.

These two goals are not necessarily synonymous. As you may already know, what your boss thinks about you and who you are may be two different things. The first job of anyone who wants to become a superstar is to actually start doing more valuable work. The second job is to gradually let your boss (and your boss' bosses) know that.

Make that commitment now.

Then make a list of all the ways you are currently valuable to your boss. And then make another list of things you can do to increase your value.

That list will be a good source of ideas for you. Let's say you implement this plan at the start of the year. In January, for example, you might make it a point to get your boss his most important report a day earlier than normal. In February, you might tell him he can delegate to you the sales calls he hates to make.

If you use a daily task list, you should be making great progress by the spring and have completely upgraded your responsibilities by the middle of the year. Now is the time to start letting your boss know about your achievements (in the event that he hasn't noticed already).

Guide all of your business decisions by one sole criterion: How will this action help my company increase its long-term profitability?

Meanwhile, be sure to stay humble and credit other people for their assistance when they have, in fact, helped you.

Be conscious of your boss' ego, too. Give him credit whenever anyone compliments you on some achievement. A statement as simple as "I couldn't have done it without Jeff's help/wisdom" will usually do the trick.

And take the time to write your boss and key fellow employees the occasional memo thanking them for their help.

By following a two-tier strategy – contributing more to the business and making friends along the way – you will ensure that your path to success will be quick and easy.

As your responsibilities increase, your boss will begin to depend on you.

Eventually – and this may happen in six months, or it may take a year – he will see you as an entirely different and more important employee than any of the others he deals with. He will begin to think of you as *indispensable*.

At that point, you should have no trouble getting your 10% raise. You might do much better than that.

S&A: Is there anything else an employee should do to make sure they get that raise?

Ford: Yes... and it's very important not to skip this step.

Establish relationships with other employees who have a higher rank than you. Ask them for their help and insight. Volunteer to help them do their jobs, and do that work after hours.

Your goal is to develop a back-up network of powerful people who see you as an up-and-comer. These people can be instrumental in getting you the raise you deserve if your boss, for whatever reason, fails to give you your due.

If you can, develop relationships with colleagues from other businesses in your industry, too. You never know – a few of them may offer you more than 10% to come and work for them.

Here's a key point: The habits you have to work on now in order to get yourself that 10% raise will be the same habits that will help you double or triple your salary in the future. Superstar employees don't do a hundred things better than ordinary, good employees. They usually do just a handful. You'll discover and perfect your handful next year in seeking to please your boss, and you'll be able to use those new skills to go all the way to the top.

S&A: But what if the actions you have to take to please your boss are not the best thing for the business?

Ford: I receive this question often. Some businesses – and this happens more frequently with larger, corporate businesses than with growing enterprises – become politically divided. In such businesses, it's possible to get a job working for someone who cares more about himself and his own power than about the company's future.

If you have such a boss, you should really try to find a better one. But if you can't, you will have to be a bit duplicitous. You will have to do everything you can to please him while you are carrying out your plan. But at the same time, find someone else in the company, someone with power, who is willing to mentor you.

That person will be either one of your boss' equals or one of his bosses. Most importantly, he must be someone who is committed to the company's long-term profitability. Remember, that is the bottom-line measuring stick for the success of any business.

Work to please your mentor at the same time as you work to please your boss. By pleasing your boss, you'll get your big raise next year. And by pleasing your mentor, you eventually will be able to abandon your boss' rotten ship and secure a much better position.

S&A: All great advice. Any closing thoughts?

Ford: The greater your contribution to your company's success, the higher the salary you will demand. And the best way to be a big contributor is to practice a financially valuable skill.

There aren't a whole lot of financially valuable business skills to choose from. Though it's good to know how to analyze a spreadsheet or engineer a new design, if you want to make dramatically more money than you're making now, you are almost certainly going to have to start doing at least one of the three things businesses traditionally pay big bucks for: selling, marketing, and/or managing profits.

You've probably heard this before... and you might be thinking this advice does not apply to you because you don't work in a sales or marketing role.

That's not the case at all...

You don't need to change your profession to contribute a financially valuable skill to your employer. While you work as an accountant or lawyer or engineer, work also with the sales and marketing team to find out how you can help them.

Do this voluntarily. Make friends and connections. Do honest and good work for them. Eventually, you will be seen as someone who can step up to take a senior position.

I know two accountants, three lawyers, and one engineer who did that. I also know a data input operator, a proofreader, and a customer service person... they are all CEOs or COOs today making hundreds of thousands with seven-figure net worths...

But even if you choose not to do that, you can and should be able to boost your salary by 10% next year. And here is how you are going to do it:

First, make a resolution to be more valuable to your boss and/or your business. Do it now. Write it down.

Second, make a list of all the ways you are currently valuable to your boss and/or your business.

Third, make a list of a dozen or so ways that you can increase your value to your boss and/or your business. And pick at least one of them as your objective for next month.

And fourth, figure out some way to communicate to your boss or to your company's president that you want to make a bigger contribution this year. (No need to tell him you want a higher salary. He will "get" that without your saying so.)

If you set for yourself the goal of getting a 10% raise next year and you get just half of that, you will still be much richer when you retire than you will be if you ignore this advice and go back to accepting the ordinary.

So please – start with that 10% goal. Decide to be a much better employee in six months and have a network of people in place who understand your value in one year.

Then get that raise and watch your wealth grow.

S&A: This is all very useful information. Thanks, Mark.

Ford: You're welcome.

Summary: To get a raise at work, first, make a commitment to become the most valuable employee in your department in six months. Second, become the most valuable employee in your boss's view in one year. Third, establish relationships with other employees who have a higher rank than you. The habits you have to work on now in order to get yourself that 10% raise will be the same habits that will help you double or triple your salary in the future.

THE GREATEST FINANCIAL GIFT YOU CAN GIVE TO YOUR CHILDREN

This interview is for your children and grandchildren.

You've probably heard about America's huge debt load. The U.S. government's debt exceeds $16 trillion – which breaks down to around $140,000 per household. And this burden will fall on the youngest Americans. It's unethical. It's unfortunate. But it's the reality.

With this giant financial obligation bearing down on them, Tom Dyson, publisher of *Common Sense Publishing*, says it's critical that right now your children and grandchildren learn about money and finance. But they don't teach finance in schools. If you don't teach them this knowledge, no one will.

Read on to learn the financial concepts your kids have to know to survive in the years ahead.

Stansberry & Associates: Tom, why do you think it's so important for our children to learn finance?

Tom Dyson: If our children are financially illiterate, they have as much chance as survival in the years ahead as a swordsman in a gunfight. There will be no mercy for the financially illiterate in the future. It's likely these people will live as indentured servants to the government and its creditors.

But if our kids have a grasp of finance and its basics – and they obey its laws – they will grow up rich. They will be in a position to help other Americans, too.

S&A: So how can parents go about teaching their kids finance?

Dyson: There are three vital financial concepts all children need to understand. I hope our readers pass them on to their children and grandchildren as soon as they can. I have two young children... And these three concepts are my starting point for their financial education.

S&A: Can you walk us through these concepts and how to teach them to our kids? Let's start with the first concept.

Dyson: Sure. The first concept our kids must know is that they are not entitled to money or wealth... or anything for that matter, even Christmas presents. They must earn money. I want my children to learn that they shouldn't expect anything to be handed to them. I don't want them to rely on the government for their livelihood, like many people do right now.

So many people treat money and prosperity as an entitlement. The government even calls its welfare programs "entitlements." This word – and what it represents – gets stamped into young people's brains. Kids act as if they are somehow entitled to toys, video games, and cars. But why should they be? Just because they have parents, it doesn't mean they should get everything they want... or anything at all, for that matter.

I plan to regularly remind my children of this when they are old enough to understand it. And I'm not going to pay my kids an allowance. An allowance would reinforce the sense of entitlement. They can make money by earning it: doing the dishes, making their beds, mowing the lawn... there are a million things. My wife and I will pay them for doing those things. But I'm not going to just give them money.

S&A: So after our children learn they're not entitled, what's the next concept they have to know?

Dyson: The second concept children need to understand is debt. Debt is expensive. If you abuse it, it will destroy you. Like the entitlement mentality, debt is an enslaver. It robs you of your independence. I avoid debt in my personal life... and when I'm choosing investments.

S&A: A lot of people have trouble visualizing the true cost of debt. Can you give us an example?

Dyson: The best way to illustrate the cost of debt is to calculate the total amount of interest the debt generates in dollars over the lifetime of the loan, instead of looking at the interest rate (like most people do). Once you look at it like that, you can see how expensive borrowing money really is.

For example, say you borrow $100,000 with a 30-year mortgage at 7%. Over 30 years, you'll end up paying $140,000 in interest to the bank. In the end, you're out $240,000 for a house that cost less than half that. Not a good deal.

S&A: Not at all. What's the third concept we need to teach our kids?

Dyson: The third thing our kids need to learn is the power of compound interest and the best way to harness it.

Compound interest is the most powerful force in finance, and it's an incredibly powerful idea for children to understand. It is the force behind almost every fortune. The brilliant Richard Russell calls compound interest "The Royal Road to Riches." And it's mathematically guaranteed.

S&A: Can you give us an example of how it works?

Dyson: Let's say you have $100 earning 10% annual interest. At the end of a year, you'll have $110. During the second year, you'll earn interest on $110 instead of $100. In the third year, you'll earn interest on $121... and so on. This is the power of compound interest. The numbers get enormous over time, simply because you're earning interest on your interest.

S&A: And why do you say this idea is especially important for children to understand?

Dyson: Because time is the most important element in compounding, children have the ultimate edge in the market: the time to compound over decades.

S&A: Where's the best place to put compounding to work?

The stock market is the best place to earn compound interest. You buy companies that have 50 years or more of rising dividend payments ahead of them. Then you let the mathematics work.

As soon as my kids are old enough to understand some arithmetic, I am going to sit down with the classic compounding tables and show them which stocks they have to buy. I'll use Coca-Cola, Johnson & Johnson, and Philip Morris as examples.

After that, assuming they have the discipline to follow through, **they *will* get rich**. There's no doubt about it.

S&A: Great points. Any final thoughts?

Dyson: You have the responsibility to educate your kid about finance. If you don't, no one else will, and they will suffer for it.

Encourage them to work hard and avoid the entitlement mentality. Teach them the power of compound interest and explain the dangers of debt.

If you do this, you will equip your kids and grandkids to survive financially in the difficult circumstances ahead. You'll provide them with something that nobody can place a price on: the power of independence.

S&A: Sounds good. Thank you, Tom.

Dyson: My pleasure.

Summary: There are three concepts your children and grandchildren have to learn if they want to survive in the future. They need to know how to be independent, why debt is dangerous, and how to grow money. And remember, if you don't give them this knowledge, no one else will.

OPTIONS, TRADING, AND SHORT-TERM INVESTING

THE 5 MAGIC WORDS EVERY TRADER SAYS OVER AND OVER

When presented with a potential investment opportunity, the great investor instinctively says five simple words.

These words work with real estate investing, small business investing, blue-chip stock investing, or even short-term trading. And they're the secret to getting rich in the markets.

Read on to learn the five magic words every great trader says over and over, all the time.

Stansberry & Associates: Brian, you claim "five magic words" are the secret to getting rich in the markets and through investments. You claim every rich investor or trader says these words over and over. Can you share those magic words?

Brian Hunt: Sure... The five magic words – and this works with real estate investing, small business investing, blue-chip stock investing, or even short-term trading – are: "How much can I lose?"

The rich, successful investor is always focused on how he can lose money on a deal, a stock, or an option position. He is always focused on risk. Once he has the risk taken care of, he can move on to the fun stuff... making money.

Almost everyone who is new to the markets or new to making investments is 100% about making money... the upside. They're always thinking about the big gains they'll make in the next Big Tech stock or currency trade or their uncle's new restaurant business.

They don't give a thought to how much they can lose if things don't work out as planned... if the best-case scenario doesn't play out. And the best-case scenario usually doesn't play out. Since the novice investor never plans for this situation, he gets killed.

I've found, through years of investing and trading my own money – and through years of hanging out with very successful business-people and great investors – that when presented with an idea, the great investor or trader reflexively asks early in the discussion, "How much can I lose?"

Like I say, this can be a real estate deal, a small business investment, a quick trade, a stock position, or a commodity investment. The concern is always, "How much can I lose? What happens if the best-case scenario doesn't pan out?"

S&A: It's along the lines of Warren Buffett's famous rules of successful investment. Rule one: Never lose money. Rule two: Never forget rule one.

Hunt: Right. Buffett is probably the greatest business analyst to ever live... the greatest capital allocator to ever live. He's worth over $50 billion because of his ability to analyze investments.

When they ask the old man his secret, he doesn't talk about the intricacies of balance sheets or cash flow analysis. The first thing he recommends to folks who want to make money in the market is to not lose money in the market. He's obsessed with finding out how much he could potentially lose on a stake. Once he's satisfied with that, he looks at what the upside is.

So Buffett is your great investor. Now take Paul Tudor Jones, an incredible trader with a net worth in the billions. His interview in the trading bible *Market Wizards* is the most important thing any new trader can read. His interview is filled with how he's obsessed with not losing money... with playing defense.

Tudor's famous quote is the trader's version of Buffett's investment quote. Tudor says the most important rule of trading is playing great defense, not offense.

If a new investor or trader taped Buffett's quote in a place he'd see it every day... and if he read Tudor Jones' interview once per month... and if he reflexively asks himself, "How much can I lose?" before investing a penny in anything, he'd be worlds ahead of most people out there. He'd set himself up for a lifetime of wealth.

S&A: OK, that covers the theory. How can we put "how much can I lose" into everyday practice?

Hunt: Well, if you're putting money into a startup business, a speculative stock, an option position, or anything else that is on the riskier end of the spectrum, the answer to "how much can I lose?" is usually, "Every last dollar."

While speculative situations can be tremendous wealth-generators, they're best played with small amounts of your overall portfolio. Or if you're a conservative investor, not played at all. Let's say you're buying a speculative gold-mining stock or a speculative tech company with just one potential "big hit" product.

With speculative positions, there is always the possibility that your money could evaporate. This is where the concept of position sizing comes into play. In a speculative situation, you're going to want to put just 0.5% or just 1% of your overall portfolio into that idea. That way, if the situation works out badly, you only lose a little bit of money. You certainly don't want to put 5% or 10% of your portfolio into a speculative position. That's way too big.

S&A: How about advice for conservative investors?

Hunt: I think conservative investors should stick to Warren Buffett-type investments... owning incredible companies with great brand names, like Johnson & Johnson or Coca-Cola. These are the safest, most stable companies in the world.

When you buy companies like this at cheap prices, when they are out of favor for some reason, it's very hard to lose money on them. They are such incredible profit generators that their share prices eventually rise and rise.

My friend and colleague Dan Ferris, who writes our Extreme Value advisory, provides advice on how and when to buy these dominant companies better than anyone in the business. He knows exactly what they are worth... and he watches them like a hawk to find the right buy-points for his readers.

If a conservative investor can buy a super world-dominating company like Johnson & Johnson or Coca-Cola or Intel for less than eight or 10 times its annual cash flow, it's very hard to lose money in them. Eight to 10 times cash flow is often a hard floor for share prices of elite businesses. They don't go down past that.

S&A: How about the concept of "replacement cost"? Do you think that's important in the quest to not lose money?

Hunt: A while back, I had lunch with a successful professional real-estate investor who raved about some of the values he found on the east coast of Florida.

The market was wrecked there. There are a lot of sellers who needed to dump right then and ask questions later... So he's found tons of properties that are selling for less than the cost it would take to build the structures if they weren't there in the first place. He's bought properties for less than that rock-bottom value... for less than replacement cost.

Since he is focusing on not losing money... and buying below replacement cost... it's going to be easy for him to make money on his properties. Mind you, he's not raving about price-appreciation potential. His eyes lit up because his downside was so well-protected.

That's the mindset the new investor needs to cultivate. He needs to realize the time to start raving is when he's found a situation where it's going to be difficult for him to lose a lot of money. The upside will take care of itself.

S&A: How about commodities? I know you like to trade commodity stocks.

Hunt: Oh, I love to trade commodity-related stocks... copper producers, oil-service companies, uranium, gold, silver, agriculture. They boom and bust like crazy. And you can make money both ways. I like to say they are "well behaved."

The key to not losing money – which leads to making terrific money – in commodity stocks is to focus your buying interest in commodities that have been blown out... that are down 60% or 80% from their high. Find commodities that have suffered brutal bear markets. The longer the bear market, the better. This is the time that the risk has been wrung out of them.

Every commodity has what's called a "production cost." This is how much it costs to produce a given unit of that commodity. It's similar to the concept of "replacement cost."

After a big bear market in a commodity, you'll often find it trading for below its replacement cost. Sentiment toward the asset will be so bad that nobody wants it. So producers get out of the business... and demand for that commodity increases because it is so cheap. This sows the seeds of a big bull market.

But to get back to covering your downside in commodities, focus on markets that have suffered a terrible selloff or bear market. In these situations, the answer to "how much can I lose?" is often, "Not much... It's already selling at rock-bottom levels."

You can certainly make money in commodities that have been trending higher for a long time, but the sure way to not lose money is to focus on the commodities that have absolutely been blown out.

Gold and gold stocks were a classic case of this in 2001. Gold and gold stocks were such bad investments for so long that everyone who bought in the 1980s or '90s had sold their holdings in disgust. They finally got so cheap and hated that they couldn't go any lower. Then they skyrocketed.

S&A: Good advice... Any parting shots?

Hunt: When you start out in this game, you're as bad as you're going to get. So take supertrader Bruce Kovner's advice and "undertrade."

Make really small bets to get the hang of things... to get the hang of handling your emotions. If you have $10,000 to get started, set aside $7,000 and trade with $3,000 for the first six or 12 months.

But even after going through a training period like this, it's tough to learn not to lose money unless you actually feel the pain of losing a lot of money. It took me touching several very hot stoves and suffering several big losses early on in my career before I learned this.

If I am a skilled trader and investor nowadays, it is only because I have made every boneheaded mistake you can think of and learned not to repeat it. I've learned that you can make great money in the market simply by not making stupid mistakes... by playing great defense.

S&A: Winning by not losing. It works for Buffett and Paul Tudor Jones... So it's probably worth focusing on. Thanks for your time.

Hunt: My pleasure.

Summary: When presented with an idea, the great investor or trader instinctively asks, "How much can I lose?" Once you're satisfied with how much you can lose, then look at what the upside is. It's winning by not losing... and it's the mindset every new investor needs to cultivate.

POSITION SIZING

The following interview is one you'll want to print out and read again and again until it becomes second nature.

It's one of the most important ideas any investor can learn. It's an essential element of success for everyone, from the conservative novice investing for retirement to the professional short-term trader. Ignoring this idea is responsible for more losses than any other investment mistake.

To explain this idea, we welcome Brian Hunt. Brian is a successful private investor and trader, and the Editor in Chief of Stansberry & Associates Investment Research, one of the country's largest independent financial publishing firms.

If you're looking to take your investing or trading to the next level, you must master this idea.

Stansberry & Associates: Brian, one of the most important things any new investor can learn is correct position sizing. Can you define the idea for us?

Brian Hunt: Sure... Position sizing is an incredibly important part of your investment or trading strategy. If you don't know the basics of this concept, it's unlikely you'll ever succeed in the market. Fortunately, it's an easy concept to grasp.

Position sizing is the part of your investment or trading strategy that tells you how much money to place into a given trade.

For example, suppose an investor has a $100,000 account. If this investor buys $1,000 worth of shares in company ABC, his position size would be 1% of his total capital. If the investor bought $3,000 worth of stock, his position size is 3% of his total capital.

Many folks think of position size in terms of how many shares they own of a particular stock. But the successful investor thinks in terms of what percentage of their total account is in a particular stock.

S&A: Why is position sizing so important?

Hunt: Position sizing is the first and probably most important way investors can protect themselves from what's known as the "catastrophic loss."

The catastrophic loss is the kind of loss that erases a large chunk of your investment account. It's the kind of loss that ends careers... and even marriages.

The catastrophic loss typically occurs when a trader or investor takes a much larger position size than he should. He'll find a stock, commodity, or option trade he's really excited about, start dreaming of all the profits he could make, and then make a huge bet.

He'll place 20%, 30%, 40% or more of his account in that one idea. He'll "swing for the fences" and buy 2,000 shares of a stock instead of a more sensible 300 shares. He'll buy 20 option contracts when he should buy three.

The obvious damage from the catastrophic loss is financial. Maybe that investor who starts with $100,000 suffers a catastrophic 80% loss and is left with $20,000. It takes most folks years to make back that kind of money from their job.

But the less obvious damage is worse than losing money... It's the mental trauma that many people never recover from. They can get knocked out of investing forever. They just stick their money in the bank and stop trying. They consider themselves failures. They see years of hard work – as represented by the money they accumulated from their job or business – flushed down the toilet. It's a tough "life pill" to swallow. Their confidence gets shattered.

So clearly, you want to avoid the catastrophic loss at all costs... And your first line of defense is to size your positions correctly.

S&A: What are the guidelines for choosing a position size?

Hunt: Most great investors will tell you to never put more than 4% or

5% of your account into any one position. Some professionals won't put more than 3% in one position. One percent, which is a much lower risk per position, is better for most folks.

Seasoned investors may vary position size depending on the particular investment. For example, when buying a safe, cheap dividend stock, a position size of up to 5% may be suitable. Some managers who have done a ton of homework on an idea and believe the risk of a significant drop is nearly non-existent will even go as high as 10% or 20% – but that's more risk than the average investor should take on.

When dealing with more volatile vehicles – like speculating on junior resource stocks or trading options – position sizes should be much smaller... like a half a percent... or 1%.

Unfortunately, most novices will risk three, five, or 10 times as much as they should. It's a recipe for disaster if the company or commodity they own suffers a big, unforeseen move... or when the market in general suffers a big unforeseen move. These big, unforeseen moves happen with much greater frequency than most folks realize.

S&A: Can you explain how the math works with position sizing?

Hunt: Yes... But first I need to explain a concept that goes hand in hand with determining correct position sizing: protective stop losses.

A protective stop loss is a predetermined price at which you will exit a position if it moves against you. It's your "uncle" point where you say, "Well, I'm wrong about this one, time to cut my losses and move on."

Most people use stop losses that are a certain percentage of their purchase price. For example, if a trader purchases a stock at $10 per share, he could consider using a 10% stop loss. If the stock goes against him, he would exit the position at $9 per share... or 10% lower than his purchase price.

If that same trader uses a stop loss of 25%, he would sell his position if it declined to $7.50 per share, which is 25% less than $10.

Generally speaking, a stop loss of 5% is considered a "tight stop"–

that is close to your purchase price – and a 50% stop loss is considered a "wide stop" – that is a long way from your purchase price.

Combining intelligent position sizing with stop losses will ensure the trader or investor a lifetime of success. To do this, you need to understand the concept many people call "R."

S&A: Please explain...

Hunt: "R" is the value you will "risk" on any one given investment. It is the foundation of all your position-sizing strategies.

For example, let's return to the example of the investor with a $100,000 account. We'll call him Joe.

Joe believes company ABC is a great investment, and decides to buy it at $20 per share.

But how many shares should he buy? If he buys too many, he could suffer a catastrophic loss if an accounting scandal strikes the company. If he buys too little, he's not capitalizing on his great idea.

Here's where intelligent position sizing comes into play. Here's where the investor must calculate his R.

R is calculated from two other numbers. One is total account size. In this case, it's $100,000. The other number is the percentage of the total account you'll risk on any given position.

Let's say Joe decides to risk 1% of his $100,000 account on the position. In this case his R is $1,000. If he decided to dial-up his risk to 2% of his entire account, his R would be $2,000. If he was a novice or extremely conservative, he might go with 0.5%, or an R of $500.

Joe is going to place a 25% protective stop loss on his ABC position. With these two pieces of information, he can now work backwards and determine how many shares he should buy.

Remember... Joe's R is $1,000, and he's using a 25% stop loss.

To calculate how large the position will be, the first step is to *always* divide 100 by his stop loss.

In Joe's case, 100 divided by 25 results in four. Now, he performs the next step in figuring his position size. He then takes that number – four – and multiplies it by his R of $1,000.

Four times $1,000 is $4,000, which means Joe can buy $4,000 worth of ABC stock... or 200 shares at $20 per share.

If ABC declines 25%, he'll lose $1,000 – 25% of his $4,000 – and exit the position.

That's it. That's all it takes to practice intelligent position sizing.

Here's the calculation again:

100 divided by your stop loss equals "A."

"A" multiplied by "R" equals position size.

Finally, position size divided by share price equals the number of shares to buy.

Now... what if Joe wants to use a tighter stop loss – say 10% – on his ABC position? Let's do the math...

* 100 divided by 10 equals 10.

* 10 multiplied by $1,000 equals $10,000.

* $10,000 divided by the same $20 share price equals 500 shares.

So you can see that using a tighter stop loss with the same R allows Joe to buy a larger number of shares, while risking the same amount of his total account... $1,000.

Next, let's say Joe wants to use a super-tight stop loss of just 5% on his position. In this case, if ABC declines just 5% to $19 per share, he's out of the trade.

This tighter stop loss means he can buy even more shares. Let's do the math again...

* 100 divided by 5 equals 20.

* 20 multiplied by $1000 equals $20,000.

* $20,000 divided by the $20 share price equals 1,000 shares.

Again, a tighter stop loss with the same R of $1,000 means he can buy twice as many shares and still risk the same amount of his total account.

As you can see, you can use the concepts of position sizing and stop losses to determine how much of any asset to buy... from crude oil futures to currencies to microcaps to Microsoft.

If you're trading a riskier, more volatile asset, the stop-loss percentage should typically increase and the position size should decrease.

If you're investing in a safer, less volatile asset, the stop-loss percentage should decrease and the position size should increase.

And like I mentioned earlier, a good, "middle of the road" R that will work for anyone is 1% of your total account. Folks new to the trading game would be smart to start with half of one percent of their account. This way, you can be wrong 10 times in a row and lose just 5% of your account.

S&A: Any closing thoughts?

Hunt: Again, the biggest thing intelligent position sizing does is keep you from suffering the catastrophic loss. The golden rule of investing or trading is, "Don't lose money." Intelligent position sizing ensures you always follow rule number one.

S&A: Thanks for talking with us.

Hunt: My pleasure.

Summary: Position sizing is your first line of defense against catastrophic loss. Combining intelligent position sizing with protective stop losses will ensure the trader or investor a lifetime of success.

"BAD TO LESS BAD" TRADING

In this interview, Brian Hunt, Editor in Chief of Stansberry & Associates, discusses one of the most powerful ideas in investing. An idea he calls "the single greatest strategy on the planet."

This idea has probably created more investment fortunes than any other in history. It's a favorite of some of the world's richest and most successful investors. Yet it's so simple, even a child could understand it.

Read on to learn more about why this strategy is so powerful, and how you can begin to use it in your own investing immediately...

Stansberry & Associates: S&A has made an art form out of "bad to less bad" trading. Can you define the term and walk us through how it works?

Brian Hunt: "Bad to less bad" is a term my colleague Steve Sjuggerud coined years ago to describe extreme contrarian trading.

It amounts to finding assets that have been hammered for some reason... be it a natural disaster, a broad market selloff, or a long industry downturn... buying them after the market has bottomed, and making tremendous returns when a bit of normalcy returns to the market – or when conditions get "less bad" for the industry.

It's the single greatest trading strategy on the planet.

S&A: Why can the gains get so big?

Hunt: When an asset suffers a major selloff... or has suffered through an extended bear market... people say things are "bad" for that asset. Nobody wants to buy it.

Mention the asset to someone at a cocktail party and they will recoil in disgust. You'd never see it on a mainstream magazine cover, because the publishers know having that particular asset on their cover would gross out readers and potential newsstand buyers.

It's around this time – when most folks can't stand the thought of buying that asset – that it can start trading for less than its real, intrinsic value. It will start trading for less than its replacement value.

For example, if most folks hate a particular real estate market, houses in that market might start changing hands for well below the cost it would take to build new ones. This is called "trading below replacement cost."

In this kind of "bad" condition, you can often buy an asset for a third or half of its book value... because nobody wants to touch it. But if you step in and buy amidst the pessimism for 50 cents on the dollar, you can double your money if just a tiny bit of optimism returns to the market and sends the asset back to its book value. Mind you, it doesn't take great news to double the price of a cheap, hated asset... it just needs things to go from "bad to less bad."

But the great part of "bad to less bad" trading is that because of the pessimism surrounding the asset, there is little downside risk to your trade. Everyone who wanted to sell has already sold. The selling pressure is exhausted. The risk gets "wrung out" of the trade.

S&A: It sounds a lot like the famous saying from banking legend Baron Rothschild... that to make a fortune you need to "buy when there is blood in the streets."

Hunt: Exactly. It's buying near the point of maximum pessimism.

S&A: It also sounds like the "bad" conditions can be a result of a short-term hit, or the result of a long-term bear market.

Hunt: Yes. It's important to keep that aspect of "bad to less bad" trading in mind. The bad times in a particular industry could be because of a disaster, like the Gulf of Mexico blowout in 2010... or because a sector has been mired in a long bear market. Short-term or long-term, the main thing here is finding potential buys in assets that would make the average investor recoil in fear or disgust.

S&A: Give us an example of "bad to less bad" trading with the long-term condition in mind.

Hunt: Let's start with gold stocks.

Gold enjoyed a tremendous bull market in the 1970s... and reached a speculative peak in 1980. It then crashed and spent two decades mired in a terrible bear market. Gold fell from a peak of $800 an ounce in 1980 to around $250 in 2000.

The global economy generally did well in the '80s and '90s, so folks were much more interested in owning stocks and bonds than gold or gold stocks, which are typically seen as "safe haven" assets... they are seen as trades that do well in times of economic turmoil.

When an asset spends that many years in a bear market, folks "give up" on it. In gold's case, nobody wanted to own gold for over 15 years. Nobody wanted to invest in a gold mine for over 15 years. Most folks just wanted a hot technology stock. There was extreme pessimism towards gold in the late 1990s and early 2000s. Everyone had sold their gold stocks. It was the definition of "bad." Many gold stocks traded for well under the replacement cost of their mines... or even worse, less than the value of the cash they held on their balance sheets.

In 2001, things started getting "less bad" in the gold business. Gold moved off its bottom of $250 and climbed 50% in just over two years. These were the early years of folks flocking towards "real assets" like gold, silver, and oil, in response to the declining U.S. dollar. Gold advanced to $500 an ounce by 2006. It advanced to $1,000 an ounce by 2008. Gold stocks staged an incredible "bad to less bad" rally. Elite gold companies like Royal Gold and Goldcorp climbed more than 1,000% during these years. They were at depressed levels. When things got "less bad," they soared.

S&A: How about some short-term examples?

Hunt: The March 2009 panic bottom is a great example. Back then, many folks were worried we were headed for the Great Depression Part II. Credit had seized up. Stocks, real estate, bonds, and commodities had all collapsed. It wasn't just "bad" in most people's eyes. It was "horrible."

If you had stepped in and bought great stocks during this "bad" time – this time of blood running through the streets – you could have made 200% in a company like Apple in just a few years. You could have made 500% or 1,000% buying world-class resource stocks. You could have made 60% on a blue-chip company like Intel in just over a year. Everything was depressed back then... so when things got "less bad," they shot higher like a coiled spring.

S&A: You mentioned disasters can create "bad to less bad" opportunities. Can you give us an example of this?

Hunt: Well, the Gulf of Mexico disaster of 2010 is a good example I mentioned earlier.

It was a horrible situation with the worst headlines an oil company could imagine. People died when the rig blew up. Thousands of barrels of oil were spilling into the gulf every day. The containment efforts were ineffective.

The market's reaction to the whole thing was to hammer the share prices of many of the world's best oil producing and drilling companies. Even companies with modest business exposure to a drilling moratorium fell 50% in just a few months. BP, the majority owner of the well, fell 55%. Transocean, the drilling company that owned the rig, fell more than 50%. Drilling companies started selling for discounts to their book values... or absurdly cheap earnings multiples... like four or five times earnings. It was a "bad" situation.

But for investors and traders who know "bad to less bad" trading, it was an opportunity to buy great companies at discounted prices. Transocean rallied 90% off its bottom. BP rallied 80%. Again, these stocks were so deeply depressed by all of the negativity, they were like coiled springs... ready to shoot higher when things got just a little "less bad."

S&A: It's important to emphasize you're not saying you make the biggest gains as things go from "bad to good"... but "bad to less bad."

Hunt: Exactly. Steve Sjuggerud really drives this point home. He points out that you make the really extraordinary gains just when a glimmer of light appears. Not when the whole sun comes out. You have to be willing to get in there and buy when it feels uncomfortable. If you wait until the news gets rosy and people realize it isn't the end of the world, you're going to be too late. You're going to miss out on the big, easy, early gains. You have to buy near the point of maximum pessimism.

Just thinking about buying something in a "bad" condition might make you feel sick to your stomach. But the seasoned trader knows that feeling is often a great buy signal.

S&A: It sounds like the danger here is buying something that's "bad," and watching it get "worse."

Hunt: Yes... that's the biggest risk with this idea. A bad situation can get much worse. You can reduce the risk of loss with two things: Waiting on a bit of price confirmation, and using stop losses.

When I say "price confirmation," I mean that I like to see the price move just a little bit in the "less bad" direction. A plunging asset is like a falling safe. If you try to catch it in the air, you'll get crushed. It's best to wait for the safe to hit the ground.

I like to see the prices slammed to a bottom... then move just a bit higher from their lows. Maybe it's waiting to see a 5% move off the lows... or maybe it's waiting for the asset to reach a two-week high... or cross above a moving average. The key is waiting for the price to "confirm" your trading idea. This reduces the risk that you're buying something in free-fall.

When it comes to "bad to less bad" trading on longer-term ideas – the buying of assets that have been in long bear markets – you also want to see some sort of catalyst on the horizon that will cause the bear market to end.

For example, the catalyst that caused gold to emerge from its bear market was a big decline in the value of paper currencies... and emerging buying power from Asian countries like China and India.

You want a catalyst on the horizon to ensure you're not buying an asset that will just sit there and do nothing.

The other thing when trading "bad to less bad" situations is to use a stop loss. This is a predetermined point at which you will sell a position if it moves against you.

Nobody is right on "bad to less bad" opportunities all of the time... and using a stop loss ensures that you have a plan in place to deal with adverse conditions... and that over a lifetime of trading "bad to less bad," you make a lot of money when you are right, and lose a little bit of money when you are wrong.

S&A: Thanks, Brian.

Hunt: You're welcome.

Summary: When an asset suffers a major selloff or has endured an extended bear market, people say things are "bad" for that asset. Nobody wants to buy it. In this kind of "bad" condition, that asset can start trading for less than its real, intrinsic value... When things get "less bad," the asset can shoot higher like a coiled spring.

POSITION AUDIT

In this interview, Editor in Chief of Stansberry & Associates, Brian Hunt, discusses "a little-known secret that virtually guarantees you'll make money in the market."

It involves closely examining every holding in your portfolio, and then asking yourself, "If I wasn't in this position already, would I take it now?"

Read on to learn how this simple exercise can drastically improve your trading performance.

Stansberry & Associates: Brian... you're a believer in a rarely used trading strategy that can drastically improve a trader's performance. Something you call a "position audit."

Can you talk about this idea, and how our readers can start using this to make more money?

Brian Hunt: Sure... A position audit is something everyone with money in the market should do at least once a year. And if you're a trader who typically holds positions from two months to two years, you should do this exercise every month.

The exercise is taking a hard look at every position you have – long or short – and asking yourself, "If I wasn't in this position already, would I take it now?"

If the answer is "no" on any position, sell it immediately.

S&A: So the trader forces himself to be objective with his holdings on a regular basis.

Hunt: Exactly.

You see, lots of investors and traders struggle with admitting mistakes and taking losses early. Rather than cut losing positions early, they tend to hold onto them and say something like, "it will come back."

Or just as bad, they ignore the loser. They'll ignore a loser that is down 20% or 30% until it grows into a giant 60% or 80% loser. And of course, it's the giant losers that ruin your year... or your trading career.

It's simple human nature to try to forget your mistakes. Life is easier that way. And in many cases, forgetting painful memories and mistakes is a good thing.

For example, if an NFL quarterback has a horrible Sunday and throws five interceptions, he'd better get over it quickly... because he'll need his self-confidence to be effective in the next game.

But with trading, ignoring a mistake is like ignoring cancer. If you catch it early, it's not going to destroy you. But if you ignore it for months or years, it's going to be fatal.

Your goal with regular position audits is to force yourself to confront your mistakes... and root them out of your portfolio before they become big ones.

S&A: Do you recommend this for trades based on fundamentals or based on technical analysis?

Hunt: Both.

Let's say you buy company ABC because you think it's going to come out with a new tech gadget that will sell millions of units. If that gadget comes out and isn't a hit – let's say it only sells 20,000 units – the reason for owning that stock doesn't exist anymore. It's time to sell.

Or, let's say you buy a big dominant company, like phone maker Nokia used to be.

You think to yourself that it's going to be a good long-term holding. But, if Apple comes along with a game changing product like the iPhone that starts eating into Nokia's market share, the reason you bought that stock no longer exists. It's time to sell.

Those are two fundamental examples. Of course, a company has lots of moving parts you have to analyze. I made those examples very simple... but you get the idea.

S&A: Okay, how about a technical example?

Hunt: Let's say you short a company or a commodity because you think it has reached a top. Maybe it has bumped against a particular price level and cannot break through it... it suffers high-volume sell-offs. It cannot rally on great news. Those are technical reasons that cause some people to go short.

But let's say that after a few months the trader goes short and the stock manages to break through to a new high on strong trading volume.

Your whole case for going short months ago is no longer valid. It's staring you right in the face. But most traders just won't admit it.

They won't confront the mistake and cover the position. Inertia and denial take over at this point... and you're now holding onto a position simply because you took it a few months ago, which is a terrible reason to be in a position.

If the reason you took the position in the first place isn't there, or has drastically changed, while you are doing your audit, get rid of the thing.

S&A: I have a feeling we'd have record-breaking trading volume next week if every investor or trader decided to sell old losing stocks they've been ignoring for a long time.

Hunt: Oh, wow... Yes, you'd see an unbelievable dumping of stocks.

I've talked with folks at investment conferences who tell me they own over 100 different stocks. That's crazy. There's no way one individual can keep track of that many companies and do a good job of it. Those kinds of portfolios probably have 80 or 90 stocks where the original reasons for buying the shares are no longer there. They're simply being ignored.

Most people would rather ignore the mistakes than take steps to confront problems and become winners. But that's between them and their therapists.

The successful trader has to constantly confront – and admit – his mistakes. He has to be an objective reviewer of his ideas.

S&A: There's an extra problem with holding onto losers that is worth mentioning... It ties up money that could be deployed into new, better ideas.

Hunt: Absolutely.

For example, take someone who bought a bundle of tech stocks back in 1999 or 2000. By 2003, after years of a bear market, the trader or investor who didn't cut his losses has what's left of his money tied up in some garbage "dot com" companies.

That's money that can't be deployed in an emerging bull market, like commodities were back then. It's a double whammy. That trader is holding crap and missing out on a promising trend. It's the complete opposite of the golden rule of trading, which is "cut your losers short and let your winners ride."

S&A: Okay... so how can a trader perform this kind of audit without dumping his winners as well? Wouldn't you cut your winners short in a lot of situations?

Hunt: That's a great question. One has to be careful here. It's key to ask yourself what your original reason was for entering the position, and what your goal with the position is.

For example, let's say you're a trader who bought Intel months ago because it was super cheap at, say, eight times cash flow, and you expected the stock to pop because you thought the market would soon be willing to pay 12 times cash flow for the stock. This is a shorter-term idea for you.

Now, let's say you were right... let's say Intel has popped higher and is trading for 10 times cash flow, now. While performing your audit, you'd note that your original bullish argument is still intact. You wouldn't buy more of this position, but you wouldn't sell it. You'd hold it, and look to take profits once it hit your objective... the 12 times cash flow objective.

But let's say someone else bought Intel at the same time with a long-term holding goal of at least five years. That person would simply periodically check out Intel's position in the market and make sure the fundamental case is still solid. If it is, you'd hold the stock and look to compound for a long time.

For traders, it really does come down to holding winners when your plan is working out. Not necessarily buying more, but holding it because the trade is working out according to your plan.

The key here is placing most of your audit's focus on the losers. Those are the potential cancers in your account.

They need to be placed in an interrogation room and given the third degree. Is the fundamental story here still in place? If it's a stock that you're long, is it still a great value? Has management done anything stupid that is wrecking the company? Is the company's new gadget selling well? Is the technical picture still the same?

If the fundamental picture or technical picture has changed on one of your losers, chances are very good you'll be better off dumping it and moving that capital into cash, or another promising idea.

S&A: So how often do you conduct an audit?

Hunt: I do one at the end of each month. I typically trade with an intermediate time frame... like one to six months, so a monthly audit works for me. I usually hold four to six positions at any one time, and I'm very quick to cut losers. Oftentimes, the losers aren't around at the end of the month.

S&A: Sounds great. Thanks for talking with us, Brian.

Hunt: You're welcome.

Summary: A "position audit" involves taking a hard look at every open position you have and asking yourself, "If I wasn't in this position already, would I take it now?" If the answer is "no" on any position, sell it immediately. Every investor should do this exercise at least once a year.

JUDGING INVESTOR SENTIMENT

This idea is a favorite of legendary investors like Warren Buffett and Jim Rogers, yet it's simple enough for a third grader to understand.

Dr. Steve Sjuggerud has had tremendous success with this idea, and has used it for years to help make huge, safe returns for hundreds of thousands of his *DailyWealth* and *True Wealth* subscribers.

Read on to discover how you can begin to put it to use in your own investing. This interview is brief, but it's a useful idea that will work over your entire investing career.

Stansberry & Associates: Steve, in your 20-year career as an investor and newsletter advisor, you've made a lot of spectacular market calls and recommendations. And you've used the idea of judging investor sentiment to help you make those calls.

Can you define this idea... and discuss how people can use it to make safe investments?

Steve Sjuggerud: Absolutely. Using sentiment to find great investment opportunities comes down to going against what the majority of investors are doing. The key to using it correctly is knowing that sentiment only works at the real extremes...

When everyone can't stand the thought of owning a particular kind of investment, chances are good that it's time to buy. A great example of this situation was stocks in early 2009. Most people were selling their stocks and completely disinterested in buying more... But it was actually a fantastic time to buy. I'd personally borrowed money to buy stocks around that time – the only time I've done that in my entire career.

On the other hand, when everyone loves an asset – like when everyone loved tech stocks in 2000 – chances are good that the asset is expensive, dangerous, and due for a big fall.

S&A: Why is that the case?

Sjuggerud: It's just human nature. Most folks like to be with the crowd... That's what feels comfortable.

Most investors – even professional investors like mutual fund managers – would rather make investments that everyone else is making because that's what makes them feel comfortable and safe. Actually focusing on the value they are getting for their investment dollar is often a secondary consideration.

The trouble is, by the time everyone likes a particular investment, the big gains are already gone. It's going to be overvalued. And ironically, it's often going to be dangerous.

By the time everyone jumped into stocks in 2000, it was too late to make big gains. By the time everyone jumped into real estate in 2006, it was too late to make big gains. In both cases, the markets became horribly overpriced and eventually crashed.

S&A: So what tools can we use to measure investor sentiment?

Sjuggerud: Judging investor sentiment is just as much an "art" as it is a "science." You have to learn how to recognize extremes in investor sentiment.

S&A: Can you describe some of the ways that you gauge investor sentiment?

Sjuggerud: There's a big list of indicators that I follow... There are lots of statistical studies of investor sentiment. I've even crunched a lot of numbers myself with very expensive computer programs and data sets.

I monitor surveys of individual investors, surveys of money managers, and surveys of what newsletter advisors are saying. I also watch how much money is flowing into particular investment funds, where big hedge funds are positioned in the futures markets, and I monitor a few economic surveys... like consumer sentiment.

Each one measures a different aspect of investor sentiment... and I don't place any single one above all the others. It's about following them all, and taking the weight of the evidence into account.

My friend Jason Goepfert does a great job of monitoring many of these indicators with his SentimenTrader website, and I highly recommend his service as a "one-stop shop" for keeping a tab on investor sentiment. It's what I use.

Again, the key here is to look for situations of extreme pessimism or extreme optimism. When everyone thinks the same thing, everyone is probably wrong. The extremes are what's important.

You have to be on the lookout for situations where everyone in the room is bullish on something or bearish on something. If everyone is bullish on something, I'm going to avoid it. If everyone is bearish on something, I'm probably going to buy it.

One of smartest things super-investor Warren Buffett ever said was that "you want to be fearful when others are greedy, and greedy when others are fearful."

S&A: How do you use sentiment to invest? Do you immediately buy something just because it's hated or unloved?

Sjuggerud: No, and that's an important point... I do love using sentiment as part of my trading "edge." I love that you can't easily measure "cocktail party chatter" with an index or a computer. But just because an asset is hated or unloved or ignored Isn't enough to buy. I also like to make sure a given asset has stopped falling in price, and is starting to show a bit of an uptrend before I commit my money.

Waiting on a bit of an uptrend ensures the market is starting to recognize the opportunity I see. Waiting on the uptrend ensures I'm not sitting on "dead money," where the asset moves sideways in price for years. Hated assets can move sideways for a decade or more, especially after a huge crash like we had in tech stocks and real estate.

My recipe for making hundreds of percent gains in an investment is finding an asset that is hated or ignored, trading for a cheap price, and just starting an uptrend.

By sticking with this formula, I've been able to make big investment gains without taking much risk.

S&A: Thanks for talking with us, Steve.

Sjuggerud: You're welcome.

Summary: The key to judging investor sentiment is to look for situations of extreme pessimism or extreme optimism. When everyone thinks the same thing, everyone is probably wrong. To make hundreds of percent gains, buy an investment that is hated, cheap, and just starting an uptrend.

COMMON SENSE TECHNICAL ANALYSIS

Few investment subjects create as much confusion and controversy as technical analysis, often referred to as "chart reading." Many traders swear by its predictive value, while others regard it similarly to astrology or tarot cards.

As Editor in Chief of Stansberry & Associates and a successful private trader, Brian Hunt has reviewed just about every type of technical analysis out there. He's distilled this complex subject into a few important ideas that can be a valuable addition to any trader or investor's toolkit.

Whether you're looking to become a more successful short-term trader or just improve your long-term investing returns, we guarantee you'll find some great ideas below.

Stansberry & Associates: It's often said that out of all the ways to analyze the stock market, none generates more confusion and criticism than the practice of "technical analysis"... also known as "chart reading." Before we get into the fine details, let's define our terms.

Brian Hunt: As you said, technical analysis is often called "chart reading." It's the study of past market prices and trading volume in order to get an edge in the market.

Some folks swear technical analysis is the "Holy Grail" when it comes to profiting in stocks and commodities. They'll tell you they've found chart patterns that regularly predict huge market moves.

Some folks swear technical analysis is no different than using tea leaves and tarot cards to dictate investment decisions. They think it's all a bunch of B.S.

There's a good reason to be skeptical of most technical analysis claims. Millions of books on technical analysis and millions of dollars of technical analysis advisories have been sold over the years...

all marketed on the claim that certain gurus can predict the next big move in stocks or commodities. Just send 'em a check for $99 and you'll learn the secret. Many of these "secret formulas" are no better than flipping a coin to determine your trading direction.

But over the years, I've found there are some useful "common sense" applications of technical analysis. They can help transform ordinary traders and investors into extraordinary traders and investors. These "common sense" applications don't try to predict the future. They simply help the trader gauge where an asset is relative to the big trend... and they help the trader see how an asset's fundamentals are affecting its price.

S&A: That's the theory. Now let's cover some of these tools.

Hunt: Let's start with the most important concept in technical analysis: what a trend is.

Put simply, a *trend is a series of price movements in one general direction*. That's it. Since pictures speak louder than words, we'll use a lot of charts in this interview.

We'll start with a chart that displays an uptrend.

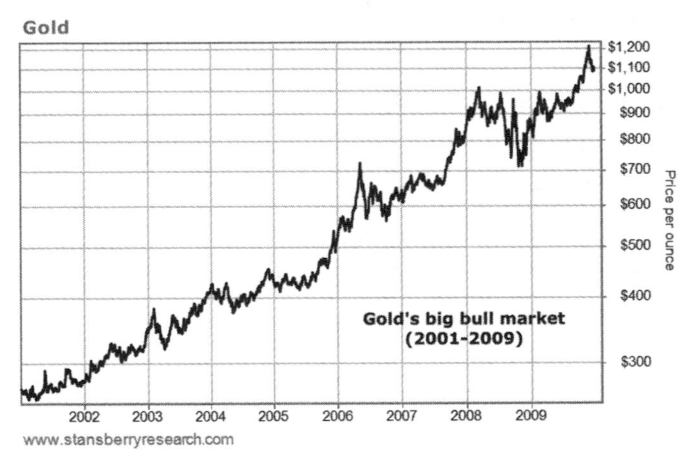

The chart above is the trend in gold prices from 2001 through 2009. You can call the price action here a "series of higher highs and higher lows." Each rally in gold takes it higher than the previous high... And each decline in gold ends a bit higher than the previous decline. That's all an uptrend is.

Let's also cover what a downtrend is. Below is the downtrend in the share price of newspaper giant Gannett, which publishes *USA Today*. This chart shows Gannett was in a downtrend from 2005 through 2008.

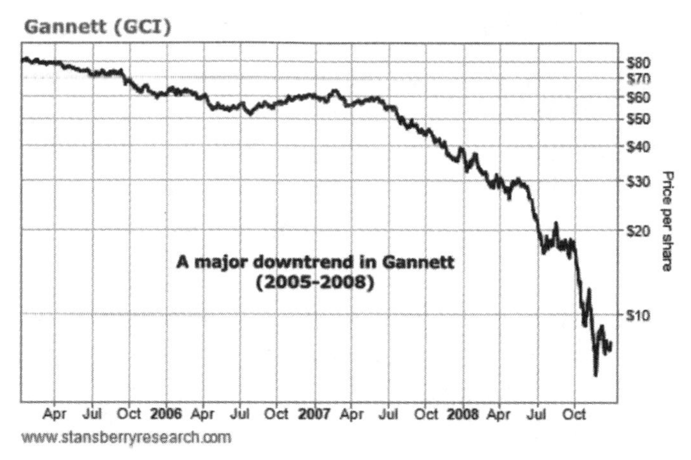

You can call this downtrend a "series of lower highs and lower lows." Each rally in Gannett's share price ends a little bit lower than the previous rally... and each decline takes Gannett a little bit lower than the previous low.

That's the key concept in technical analysis... the trend.

S&A: OK, let's move on to another concept I've heard you talk about – "respecting trends." How do you do that?

Hunt: If you don't respect trends, you'll get killed in the markets.

One of my favorite market analysts and investors of all time is Martin Zweig.

Zweig's *Winning on Wall Street* book is considered one of the greatest books ever written on the markets. He achieved fame and fortune in the 1970s and '80s with his *Zweig Forecast* market advisory. He's also a successful money manager.

Located in the middle of *Winning on Wall Street* is this timeless quote:

"I can't emphasize enough the importance of staying with the trend in the market, being in gear with the tape, and not fighting the major movements. Fighting the tape is an invitation to disaster."

In the early days of Wall Street, traders received updates by a machine that printed out prices on a roll of ticker tape. Even today, with the ticker tape machines long gone, traders still call market action "the tape." When Zweig says, "Don't fight the tape," he's really saying, "Don't fight the big trend."

Hundreds of thousands of traders have blown up their trading accounts by trading against uptrends and by trading against downtrends. Most of these traders were sure they knew something the market didn't... Maybe an uptrend was due to end in a big crash... Or a downtrend was due to end in a big rally. So, they bet on them ending.

Again, this is called "fighting the tape." And as Martin notes, it's an invitation for disaster... for the simple reason that trends tend to last longer than anyone expects them to. Or as legendary investor Jim Rogers reminds us:

"Markets often rise higher than you think is possible, and fall lower than you can possibly imagine."

This is why you never want to bet against a major uptrend or a major downtrend.

Trends can last a long time... and you must either trade with the trend, or step aside.

But never stubbornly trade against it.

From a general standpoint, *you want to be long uptrends, and short downtrends*.

And unless you are trading for lightning-fast moves of just a few days, never short a major uptrend, and never buy a major downtrend. Or in Martin Zweig's words, "*Never fight the tape*."

S&A: But you can make big money when a trend goes from up to down, and vice versa. How should a trader do it?

For example, what if you find an asset that is a terrific value and has a great bullish long-term argument for buying it, but is still locked in a downtrend? You want to buy, but you don't want to "fight the tape."

Hunt: This gets to another key concept... the art of finding tops and bottoms.

Let's start by looking at an important chart. This chart displays a type of price move that has bankrupted hundreds of thousands of people. So please pay careful attention to it.

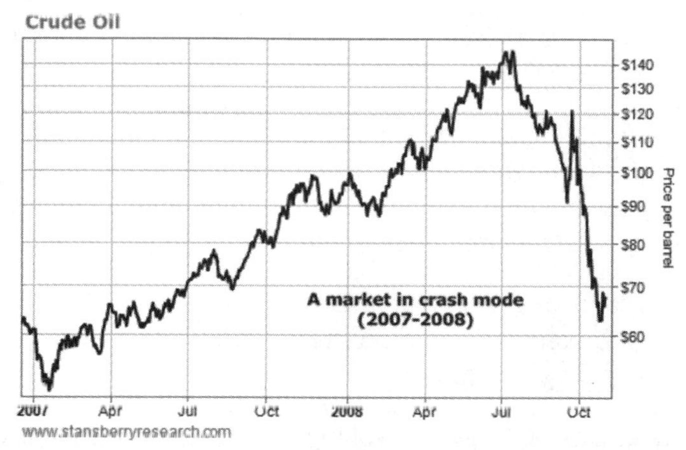

This is a chart of crude oil from early 2007 through late 2008. See that huge, sharp decline on the right-hand side? That's a market in crash mode. Some traders call this kind of move a "falling knife" or a "falling safe."

A market in such a sharp decline is nearly impossible to trade successfully. But that doesn't stop all kinds of people from trying to do so. Many people see this kind of fall and think, "*It's getting cheap. It's due for a big rebound... and I'm buying*."

Many traders get a thrill from trying to pick the exact bottom or top of a runaway market. They perform the necessary fundamental analysis to realize a market is cheap after a big fall... or expensive after a big rise. Armed with this valuation knowledge, they go for the glory and start buying... and lose a bundle.

Here's why: A huge move like the 2008 oil crash generates a lot of emotion in the marketplace. It catches most people off-guard. It causes big swings in their account values... both up and down.

All that emotion produces wild markets with little concern for fundamentals. Whether an asset is overvalued or undervalued simply doesn't matter during these moves. So saying things like, "*This stock is just so cheap*" is only going to get you and your money in trouble. It's going to get you into risky trades.

Instead of letting that sort of thing run through your head, remember that quote from Jim Rogers:

"Markets often rise higher than you think is possible, and fall lower than you can possibly imagine."

Markets are just big groups of people. People are irrational... even more so when their money is on the line and account values are jumping around like crazy. This makes trading against runaway trends – fighting the tape – a high-risk activity...

There's a much lower-risk way to trade these moves. It's a lot easier on your blood pressure... and more profitable. Let's again consider advice from Marty Zweig.

Zweig says trying to buy an asset in freefall is like trying to catch a falling safe. You'll always get squashed. His alternative is amazingly simple and profitable. Don't try to catch a falling safe. Wait for it to hit the ground... Then just walk over and pick up the money.

Let's look at crude oil again. Instead of trying to catch the falling safe by going long crude oil in October 2008 when the chart looked like this...

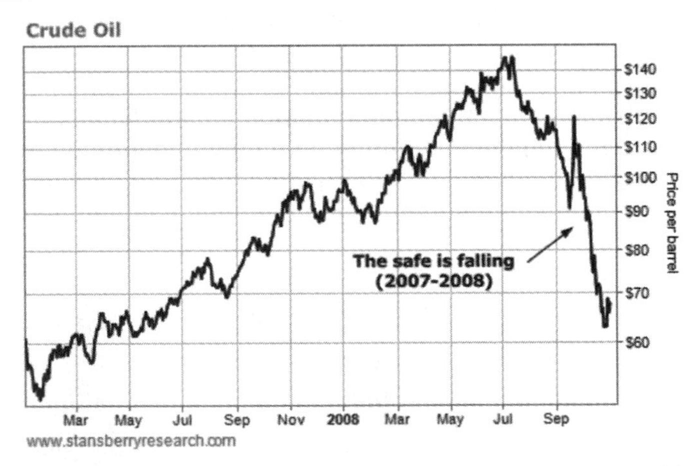

... the smart speculator waits for the safe to hit the ground. He waits for the chart to look like this...

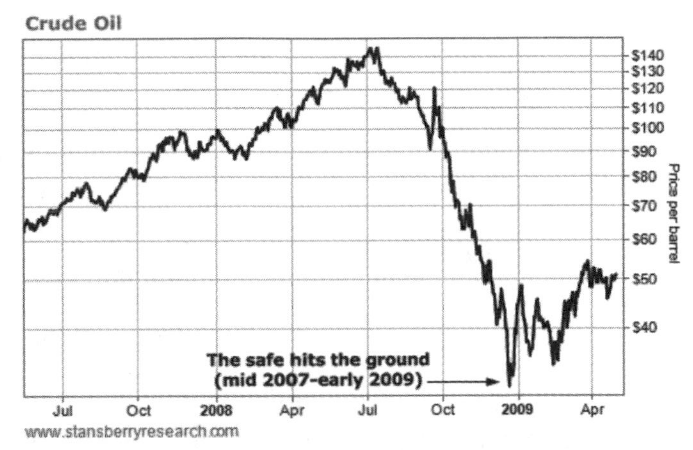

See that price action in late 2008? Traders who bought oil at $70 in October got a 50% "discount" from July's high of $140. They also lost half their money as the safe kept falling and falling. It eventually hit the ground at $35 in December.

Few market players imagined this stupendous decline could happen to crude oil. But remember Jim Rogers:

"Markets often rise higher than you think is possible, and fall lower than you can possibly imagine."

The safest time to go long crude oil and oil stocks came in February 2009. It was during this time that oil "carved out" a bottom. After hitting a low of $35 a barrel in December, oil rebounded into the upper $40 range. The oil bears countered this rally and tried to drive prices back down to the low several times. Each time, oil refused to reverse. As traders would say, oil "tested" its bottom.

At that point, it was much safer to buy oil than it was in October 2008. Anyone who went long back then was buying into a sharp decline. Traders who waited on a bottoming out process – and waited for the safe to hit the ground – made a bundle as oil went on to rally into the $70s and $80s in 2009. They waited for the trend to get exhausted... for all that emotion to get wrung out of the market. This "wringing out" process takes time... And it produces a "round bottom" like you see here:

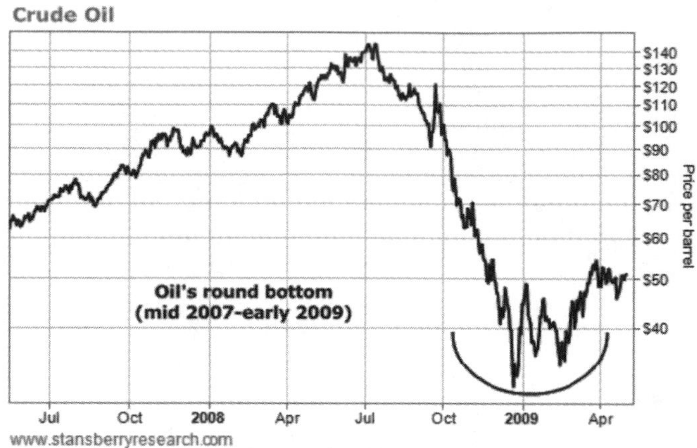

This strategy of avoiding sharp declines while trading round bottoms works for all stocks and commodities. It allows you to stand safely aside as the safe hits the ground and spills out its contents.

This line of thinking also works at market tops... and allows you to make money when assets fall. Have a look at this chart. It's one of the great moves of the 2003-2007 stock rally.

This chart shows the gigantic move Potash enjoyed from 2006-2008.

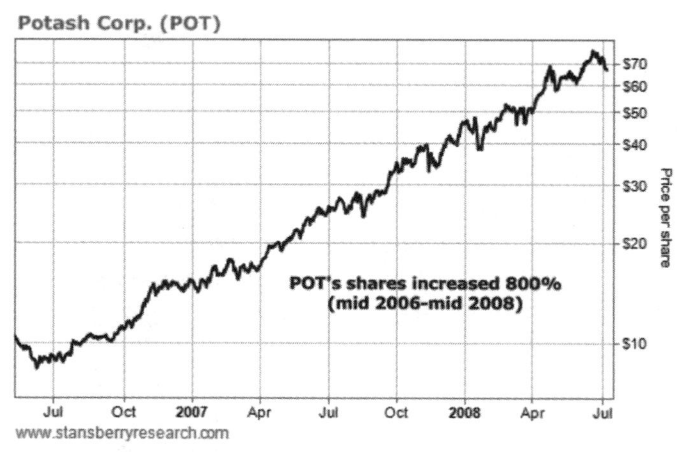

Potash is the world's largest fertilizer company. In 2006, grain and farm prices went through the roof... So fertilizer producers went through the roof as well. Potash shares increased 800% in less than two years.

After fertilizer shares ran up hundreds of percent, the investment public caught on. The news was everywhere: *Fertilizer prices are skyrocketing*! Wall Street and Main Street went wild. People were so bullish on fertilizer shares, they were willing to pay between 40 and 60 times earnings for these stocks. That's a crazy price to pay for any company... let alone for one that produces boring crop fertilizer.

So... you had two big "red flags" here. You had 1) a wildly overpriced stock, and 2) rampant bullishness from the investing public surrounding shares.

Time to go short?

No way. Look how sharp that rise is again. Sure, Potash is super-expensive and "should" suffer a big correction soon... but remember Jim Rogers:

"Markets often rise higher than you think is possible, and fall lower than you can possibly imagine."

Potash shares were still rising. The stock was a rocket ship with plenty of momentum. It was too risky to trade.

At that point, the right thing to do was place the stock on your watch list and wait for the flame at the bottom of the rocket ship to sputter out and turn cold. Here's what that "flameout" looked like:

Potash's chart had changed from a sharp uptrend to a round top. It was time to bet on the short side and let gravity do the rest.

Here's what happened over the next four months:

Gravity really worked Potash over. The stock fell 75% from its high. Short sellers made a fortune.

S&A: Let's move on to another concept: breakouts.

Hunt: In addition to knowing how to identify a trend, it's crucial the trader learns how to identify a breakout.

A breakout occurs when the price of an asset reaches either a new high point or a new low point for a given time period. An "upside breakout" is when the asset hits a new high. A "downside breakout" is when an asset hits a new low.

Breakouts can be either short-term (about five or 10 days), intermediate-term (like more than 30 days), or long-term (more than 200 days).

Breakouts serve as a starter's pistol to signal the beginning of a trend. No uptrend can start without an upside breakout... And no downtrend can start without a downside breakout. Let's look at a few examples...

After suffering the big decline of the late 2008 credit crisis, crude oil traded sideways for months before staging an upside breakout around $48 per barrel in mid-March (A). It then proceeded to drift sideways in the high $40s before staging another upside breakout around $55 per barrel in early May (B).

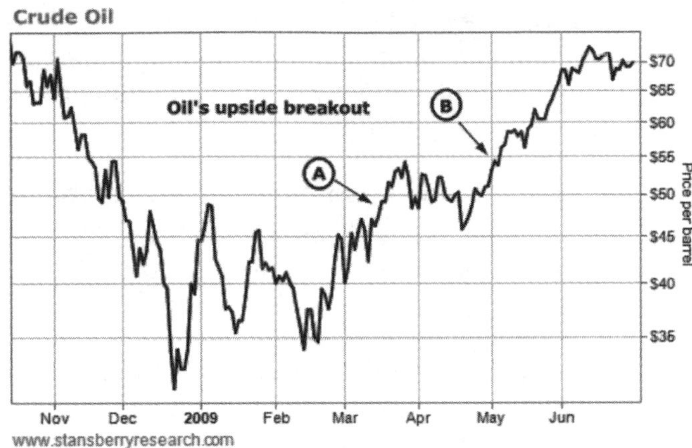

As you can see, the concept of an "upside breakout" is simple. It's when the price of an asset moves into a new area of higher prices. In oil's case, that move in early March took crude to its highest closing price of the past 60 days. Traders call that a "60-day upside breakout."

Now let's look at a downside breakout.

The chart below displays the downside breakout in shares of Potash during the summer of 2008...

After peaking at $77 in mid-June (A), Potash drifted lower into the $70-per-share range. It then staged a downside breakout in August (B)... taking shares all the way down to $51.

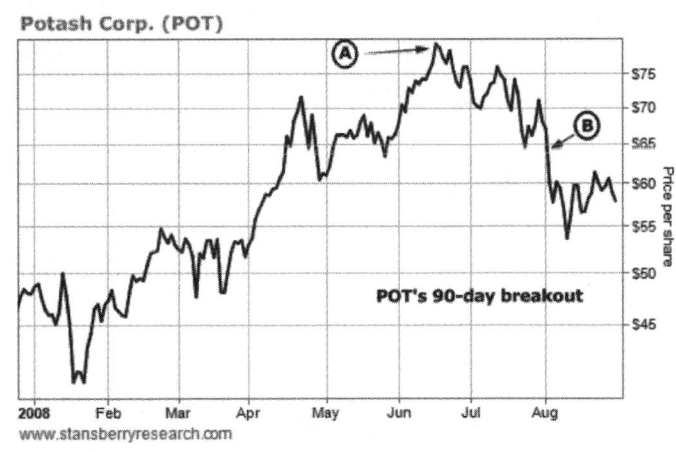

This was the lowest closing price in 90 days for Potash... So you can understand why we call this a "90-day breakout." Keep in mind... it's also a 60-day breakout, because if shares are hitting their lowest level in 90 days, they are also at a 60-day low... as well as a 30-day low and a three-day low.

Breakouts are important because they signal possible trend changes. If you are looking to trade an asset in one direction, it helps to wait on a breakout before making your move... It helps to wait for the market to "confirm" your belief.

Waiting for a bit of price confirmation ensures you aren't fighting the tape... or placing your money into assets that are drifting sideways for long periods of time.

For instance, let's say you turned bullish on crude oil in February 2009.

Waiting on that upside breakout in March ensures the market is moving in your direction. It ensures you are trading with the trend... no matter how short- or long-term your horizon. The same goes for a trader looking to bet against Potash...

Let's say you wanted to short Potash in June. You'd want to wait for a breakdown to signal a trend change before making your trade. You'd want to see some share price weakness to confirm your thesis.

Even if it's just a bit of share price weakness – say in the form of a short-term five-day downside breakout – that's considered waiting for market confirmation.

Following breakouts is no Holy Grail of trading. Breakouts can reverse in a hurry. When an asset stages a breakout in one direction, then turns right around and heads in the opposite direction soon after, it's called a whipsaw. Whipsaws are just a fact of trading life.

Below is an example of a whipsaw...

The chart above displays the share price action of oil company Suncor from mid-2008 to mid-2009.

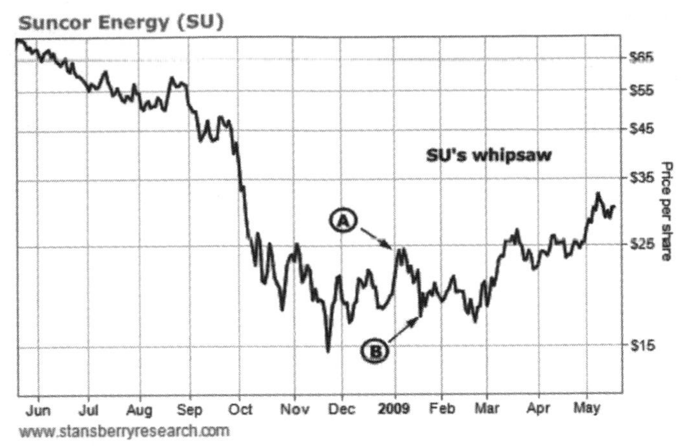

A trader bullish on Suncor might have bought shares when the stock staged a 60-day upside breakout near $22 in late December (A). That trader would have had to endure a sharp whipsaw down to $17.50 per share in the following weeks (B). Depending on where a trader has his stop loss, this whipsaw could kick him out of the trade.

Below is the same chart of Suncor, with a few more months' shown. You'll note that Suncor eventually broke out of that $22 area and ran into the high $30s (C)... but there were a few months of sideways "whipsaw action" that a trader had to deal with.

This is simply how the market works... you must deal with these situations by sticking to your protective stop loss orders... and knowing from time to time you'll have to deal with whipsaws that nearly trigger your stop losses, kick you out of trades, or produce a few months of frustration.

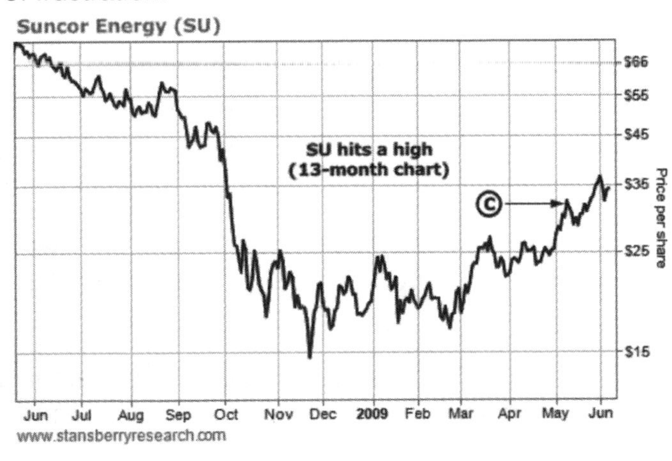

To sum things up, waiting on price breakouts – either short-term or long-term – before trading increases your odds of success because you are getting in line with the market. You're going with the tape, rather than against the tape. That's all you really need to know about this simple but critical technical concept.

S&A: What are some other common sense tools one can use to spot market tops and bottoms?

Hunt: We'd better cover "acting well" and "acting poorly." These are two more things that aren't trying to predict anything... they aren't "reading tea leaves"... they're just common sense tools that help us time trend changes. Let's go back to our Potash example from mid-2008.

Remember... back then, Potash was in the middle of a huge bull market. Shares were up 800% in two years. Tons of CNBC guests talked about how bullish they were on fertilizer stocks. You'd hear stuff like, "*Things couldn't be better for the industry*."

Retail investors across the country started hearing about high crop prices and rising fertilizer shares on the nightly news... And they started reading about them in the local paper. Food riots broke out in Mexico and Indonesia. Fertilizer companies were reporting incredible increases in revenue and profits. The Market Vectors fund family even launched a new agribusiness exchange-traded fund to capitalize on investor interest toward the sector.

Then... on July 24, 2008... Potash came out with a stunning earnings report.

Earnings came in at $905.1 million... a 220% increase from the year before, and the highest total in company history. "*This quarter established a new standard of performance for our company*," CEO Bill Doyle said. Shares fell 3.3% on massive trading volume as a result.

Yes... I said "fell," not climbed. Potash reported the greatest quarter in company history... a "new standard" in profitability... and was clobbered for it.

This horrible performance in the face of great news is what happens when a trend is changing. It's called "acting poorly"... and it's another vital technical concept to know.

As you can imagine, when an asset cannot rally in the face of wonderful news, it's a huge bearish sign for that market. It's a sign that all the great news and all the great fundamentals going for the market have been "priced in" to that market. It's a sign there aren't enough buyers in the market to help drive prices higher. They've been exhausted.

Just as it's bearish for a bull market to fall on great news, it's bullish for a bear market to rally on horrible news. Consider the case of Intel...

In April 2009, things were horrible for Intel. This was around the time of the 2008-2009 credit crisis. Many folks were worried "The Great Depression Part II" was around the corner. Intel shares fell more than 50% in four months.

Intel is the world's largest maker of semiconductors... the tiny "engines" that power the world's computers. If another Great Depression was in the cards, people wouldn't be buying computers... and Intel's business would suffer.

In mid-April, Intel reported a huge quarterly sales decline of 26% from the previous year's quarter. Profits fell 55%. Intel also offered a "blurry" outlook for the rest of the year. Wall Street hates "blurry." So what happened to Intel shares after this news? They held like a rock!

When a bear market has a bullish reaction to horrible news, that market (or stock) is said to be "acting well." It's a sign the sellers of that asset are exhausted and out of ammo. It's a sign the downtrend is likely finished.

In Intel's case, the downtrend was finished. The stock rallied 50% over the next 12 months and was one of the top-performing stocks of the year. This rally kicked off when Intel started "acting well."

To summarize, when a bull market sells off in the face of great news, it's a bearish sign. When a bear market rallies in the face of horrible news, it's a bullish sign.

S&A: OK... one more concept. Let's cover trading volume.

Hunt: That's a good one to end on. One more time, let's look at the enormous 2008 drop in shares of Potash. This situation can teach us another powerful technical concept...

The concept of trading volume.

Each day, the exchanges track the amount of trading volume in each stock index and each single security. This volume measures the amount of buying and selling activity present during the day... The higher the volume, the greater the amount of buying and selling activity.

Volume can serve as a useful tool because it allows you to track "elephants."

The stock market is dominated by large money managers... folks who run pension funds, insurance funds, mutual funds, and hedge funds. Many of these managers control billions of dollars in client assets... And when they decide to enter or exit a position, they can't do it over just a few days. They have to spread their buying over months. They even have to hire people whose main job is to determine the best way to plow big money into individual stocks.

These big money managers are the elephants in the stock market. They create the huge moves that become market trends. Remember, their portfolios can run well into the billions of dollars... So even a rich individual with a $5 million trading account is a mouse compared to these elephants.

You can track elephant behavior with trading volume.

I'm not going to say trading volume is the magic key to stock market profits. I do believe, however, that there are two tried and true guidelines for using trading volume to increase your profitability.

One is a stock experiencing heavy trading volume on down days and light trading volume on up days is being sold by the big money. The elephant tracks are pointing in the direction of lower prices.

The phenomenon of "lots of trading volume on down days, not much trading volume on up days" is sometimes called "distribution," and it's especially useful when trying to determine the end of an uptrend. Let's take a look at Potash again. We're sticking with the same time period of mid-2008... when the big uptrend ended, and eventually turned into a big downtrend.

You'll see some gray bars at the bottom of the chart below. These bars represent Potash's trading volume. Light gray bars represent days the stock advanced in price. Dark gray bars represent days the stock declined in price. The taller the bar, the greater the volume. Note that in June and July, the dark bars (days Potash declined) started to get just a bit bigger than the light bars (days Potash advanced) (A). This is an early sign that sellers have more power and more conviction than buyers.

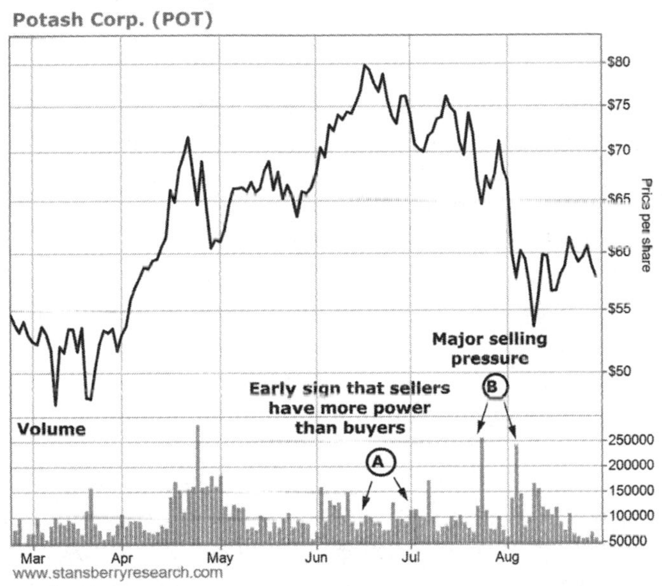

Now note the tall "skyscraper" dark bars in late July and early August (B). This is major selling pressure. Even worse, this selling pressure came on the great earnings report I just mentioned. Several elephants were fleeing Potash shares. And as you'll recall, Potash shares lost over 66% of their value soon after.

When you see a stock or stock index that was up big over the past few years start to exhibit this sort of "heavy down volume, light up volume" pattern of trading, it's a major warning sign the trend may be ending. A healthy uptrend enjoys big trading volume on buying days, not big trading volume on down days.

For our next guideline, we just flip things around and say a stock experiencing heavy trading volume on up days and light trading volume on down days is being purchased by the big money. The elephant tracks are pointing in the direction of higher prices.

The phenomenon of "lots of volume on up days, not much volume on down days" is sometimes called "accumulation," and it's especially useful when trying to determine the end of a downtrend. Perhaps the stock has fallen so much it has become an irresistible value... Or maybe the tough industry conditions hurting the business are over and large investors are taking notice.

For example, let's look at shares of Silver Wheaton from mid-2008 to early 2009.

Silver Wheaton is a company that finances early stage mining projects. It receives a slice of a project's revenue if it turns out to be a successful silver mine. Thus, the company tends to move up and down with the price of silver.

In late 2008, the price of silver crashed in response to the big 2008 credit crisis. The metal fell from $19 per ounce to $9 per ounce in less than five months. Silver Wheaton fared even worse... falling from $14 per share all the way down to $2.56. That's when the elephants started picking up shares...

On the following page is a chart of Silver Wheaton from mid-2008 to early 2009. Note the surge of buying volume in December, as represented by the series of tall gray bars (A). These are elephant tracks, and they signaled the end of Silver Wheaton's downtrend. The stock went on to gain more than 400% over the next 15 months.

Entire books have been written about volume analysis, and many traders use sophisticated formulas to track volume trends. But for the great majority of traders, these two guidelines are all you need to know about trading volume. You need to know that it often signals the end of big trends... it signals market extremes. Most of the time, this volume analysis isn't going to tell you much.

Here are the guidelines one more time: One... when an uptrend enters a period of huge selling volume, it's a sign the trend is near an end... a sign the big money is cashing in and bailing out. And two... when a downtrend enters a period of huge buying volume, it's a sign the trend is near an end... a sign the big money is seeing value and buying up shares.

S&A: That's a great set of common sense tools. Anything you'd like to leave the reader with?

Hunt: Once again... common sense technical analysis is no magic bullet. It's simply a way to help time your trades to ensure the biggest profits. Some traders have made incredible careers out of trading on advanced forms of technical analysis alone. But for most folks, it's best to "marry" basic technical concepts with fundamental measures of value. The two schools of thought can produce incredible investment results.

Summary: "Common sense technical analysis" isn't about trying to predict where an asset will go based on its chart pattern. It's simply a collection of tools that allow an investor or trader to time his decisions based on how the fundamentals are affecting prices. Married with fundamental measures of value, it can increase investment and trading returns.

HOW TO BE A "CONNOISSEUR OF EXTREMES"

In order to consistently find low-risk, high-reward trades, Stansberry & Associates recommends becoming a "connoisseur of extremes."

This strategy involves finding assets that are trading far out of their normal ranges of valuation... and subject to extreme levels of investor sentiment. For more on this timeless, common sense strategy, read the following interview with S&A Editor in Chief Brian Hunt.

Stansberry & Associates: You've mentioned in the past that to enjoy a lifetime of trading success, you've got to be able to spot "extremes" in the market... that you must become a "connoisseur of extremes."

What do you mean by that?

Brian Hunt: By saying you should become a "connoisseur of extremes," I'm saying you should always be searching for situations where a market is in a drastically different state than normal.

By locating these extreme states – and then betting on conditions returning in the direction of normal – you can consistently make low-risk profits in any type of market.

It's important to realize that extremes can occur in any market – from stocks to commodities to real estate to bonds to currencies.

Extremes can be fundamental in nature... like how cheap or how expensive a stock market is. Another name for this is a "valuation" extreme. Extremes can also be price action based... like how overbought or oversold a market is. That's a "technical" extreme. And extremes can show up in sentiment readings, like surveys that monitor investor pessimism and optimism.

S&A: Let's cover valuation extremes...

Hunt: Sure. A good example of a fundamental valuation extreme came in U.S. stocks in 1982. Back then, stocks became extremely cheap relative to their earnings power.

For U.S. stocks, the normal price-to-earnings multiple over the past hundred years or so is 16. In 1982, the economy and the stock market had been doing so poorly for so long that people simply gave up on stocks. Since nobody wanted to own stocks, they became extremely cheap. The price-to-earnings multiple fell to around 8.

It was one of the greatest times ever to buy U.S. stocks. The market rose 50% in just one year. It doubled by 1986. It rose more than 10-fold over the next 17 years.

Fast-forward about two decades and you find the opposite extreme. In 1999, optimism toward stocks was so high that the market reached a price-to-earnings ratio of 33. This was a ridiculous, extreme level of overvaluation.

Remember, the normal price-to-earnings ratio of the past 100 years is around 16. The extreme level of overvaluation made it a terrible time to buy stocks. The market crashed for several years after hitting that extreme.

When it comes to fundamentals, you need to study an asset's historical valuation and find out what's normal for that asset. When an asset gets very cheap relative to its historical valuation, you need to consider buying. When an asset gets extremely expensive relative to its historical valuation, you want to consider avoiding it... or even betting on it falling.

This goes for oil stocks, tech stocks, real estate, and lots of other assets.

S&A: OK... so people need to buy stocks when they get extremely cheap relative to their historical norm, and avoid them when they get extremely expensive relative to their historical norm. How about extremes that are "technical" in nature?

Hunt: Before we get into particulars, let's define the term to prevent confusion.

Technical analysis is the study of price action and trading volume. Many people think technical analysis is all about predicting the market, but it's not. It simply comes down to using price and volume data to gauge market action... and to help guide decisions. That's it.

There are dozens of technical indicators that measure a stock's oversold/overbought levels. One I've found useful is the "RSI," which stands for "relative strength index." The RSI is nothing magical or predictive. It's simply an objective way to gauge the overbought/oversold nature of a stock.

My colleague Jeff Clark is amazing at finding short-term technical extremes in the market. He uses an indicator called the "bullish percent index" to identify overbought/oversold extremes in broad market sectors. I'm sure Jeff will tell you there's nothing magical or predictive about the bullish percent index. Again, it's simply an objective way to gauge price action.

We are using these gauges to identify extremes in the market... then betting on the conditions being "relieved" in the other direction. When the pressure behind an extreme is released, the market tends to snap back like a rubber band stretched to its limit.

There are literally hundreds of technical indicators and chart patterns people use. While I have a handful of things that I know work, what works for me or you or someone else isn't as important as knowing the overarching goal: That you're using this stuff to spot extremes and trade them.

For example, I often trade short-term moves in blue-chip stocks, like Coke and McDonald's. These are elite businesses with tremendous competitive advantages and long histories of treating shareholders well.

But like any business, even stable blue chips go through rough patches. If they report a weak quarter or have a product recall, or any other of a dozen solvable problems, the market tends to overreact and sell the shares. The stock price will reach a state we can term "oversold." This is a condition where the stock has reached an extreme level of poor short-term price action.

It's around this time that I'll step in and trade the stock from the long side. World-class businesses have a way of rebounding from short-term setbacks. They tend to snap back from extremely oversold levels.

S&A: OK, when it comes to technical analysis, we're looking for extreme conditions that when relieved, produce "snap back" moves.

You mentioned extremes in sentiment. Let's cover that idea...

Hunt: Let's also define this term to prevent confusion. The study of market sentiment comes down to gauging the amount of pessimism or optimism toward a given asset. You can gauge the sentiment for just about any kind of asset... be it stocks, commodities, real estate or currencies.

Gauging market sentiment is more art than science. There are lots of ways to gauge sentiment that cannot precisely be measured... and some that can.

Whatever gauges you use, the goal is the same: to find extreme levels of pessimism or optimism. You want to find situations where the majority of market participants are extremely bullish or bearish... and then bet against them. You want to go against the crowd.

When most folks can't stand the thought of owning a particular kind of investment, chances are good that it's cheap... and that it's due for at least a short-term rebound.

On the other hand, when everyone loves an asset – like when everyone loved stocks in 1999 – chances are good that the asset is expensive and due for at least a short-term drop.

A few informal sentiment gauges – the kind that can't be precisely measured – are magazine covers and cocktail party chatter.

If a mainstream publication like *Newsweek* or *Time* has an asset on its cover, chances are good that the asset is far too popular, far too expensive, and due for at least a short-term drop.

Magazine publishers have to write stories lots of people want to read. Plus, it's mostly journalists – not great investors – who write those stories. Mainstream magazines are just going to write about what's popular so they can sell lots of magazines. Back in 1999 and 2000, they always had stocks on their covers. It was a danger sign. In 2006, it was all about how to cash in on the real estate boom. That was a danger sign.

The idea behind studying cocktail party chatter is similar. It's another way to get a feel for what the general public thinks about a given investment.

You can get a feel for this by talking to people at cocktail parties, family gatherings, holiday parties, and dinner parties. When lots of people are excited about a given asset and are buying as much as they can, it's a major warning sign. It's a sign the asset is too popular, too expensive, and due for a fall.

On the other hand, when most folks can't stand the thought of owning a given asset, chances are good that it's a good buy.

For example, back in 2003, I put a large portion of my net worth in gold. When I'd tell people that I owned a lot of gold, they'd look at me like I was crazy. You could say there was an extreme amount of disinterest in gold. Gold went on to rise many hundreds of percent.

S&A: What are some sentiment indicators that can be measured precisely?

Hunt: Money managers and investment newsletter writers are always being surveyed and monitored.

Just like most regular investors, the supposed professional investors get swept up in crowd following behavior. You want to bet against extremes here as well.

S&A: It sounds like being a "connoisseur of extremes" is all about finding abnormal situations, and then betting on them becoming normal again.

Hunt: Exactly. It's important to note that being a "connoisseur of extremes" – and trading them – is about getting a powerful force of nature to work in your favor. That force is called "reversion to the mean."

"Reversion to the mean" is a broad term that is used to describe the tendency for things in extreme, or abnormal, states to return to more normal states. You see "reversion to the mean" all the time. You see it in academics, business, trading, and dozens of other areas.

For example, winning an NFL Super Bowl requires an extreme set of circumstances. A football team has to have a great coach... a great set of players... and they have to play extremely well for an extended period of time. Its elite players have to avoid injury. It has to beat a series of excellent teams at the end of the season.

It's really hard to get all the stars aligned and pull off a Super Bowl-winning season. That's why Super Bowl winners tend not to win the championship the next year. They tend to "revert to the mean" and not win it.

To go back to the example of trading extremely oversold blue-chip stocks, if a blue-chip stock like Coca-Cola is sold heavily day after day for several weeks, chances are good that its trading action will "revert to the mean" and cease being so extreme. Chances are good that it will stop falling and start rising.

S&A: Understood. Any final thoughts?

Hunt: One last thing that I think is important to note is that an extreme in valuation is often accompanied by extreme technical and sentiment readings.

That's why I believe studying and trading the market with "just" fundamentals or "just" technicals can be a limiting mindset. Consider what happened with offshore drilling stocks in mid-2010, just after the terrible Gulf of Mexico oil well disaster.

After the disaster, investors dumped shares of offshore drilling stocks. They completely overreacted. It was like people believed we'd never be drilling for oil again. Sentiment toward the sector was terrible. Even companies with little business exposure to the Gulf of Mexico fell more than 30%.

This big decline left the whole sector in an extremely oversold state.

It also made the stocks very cheap. Great drilling businesses were sold down to valuations of around five times earnings.

After the selloff, you had a sector that was extremely unpopular, extremely cheap, and extremely oversold from a technical standpoint. So, I went long offshore drilling stocks and made big returns in a short amount of time.

The stocks enjoyed a sharp "snapback" rally. Again, this rally was preceded by "extreme" valuation, technical, and sentiment readings.

S&A: That's why it pays to look for extremes of all types.

Hunt: Yes, exactly.

S&A: Thanks for your time.

Hunt: My pleasure.

Summary: Being a "connoisseur of extremes" means you should always be searching for situations where a market is in a drastically different state than normal. By locating these extreme states – and then betting on conditions returning in the direction of normal – you can consistently make low-risk profits in any type of market.

PICKS AND SHOVELS

As Editor in Chief of Stansberry & Associates, Brian Hunt sees more investment ideas come across his desk in one week than most people do in five years.

As you'll see below, one of his top ways to make huge returns in booming sectors or commodities is "picks and shovels"... a "sleep at night" way to profit from a bull market.

Stansberry & Associates: For many investors, the safe, "sleep at night" way to make huge returns in booming sectors or commodities is to own the "picks and shovels" of the boom. Can you explain how this idea works?

Brian Hunt: Sure. The idea of owning "picks and shovels" in order to profit from a big sector or commodity boom simply means owning companies that supply the vital tools, products, or services many participants in the boom must use... rather than taking the riskier route and buying the individual players in the boom.

The classic success story here was back in the 1850s, when a German immigrant moved from New York to San Francisco to participate in the California Gold Rush.

Rather than taking the "all or nothing" route of looking for a big gold strike, the German immigrant sold basic goods to the miners. This was a much safer, surer way to acquire wealth than trying to find the one big strike.

The immigrant eventually started producing a new type of durable pants to sell to the miners. They became a huge hit... and the German immigrant got rich. His name was Levi Strauss. Levi didn't risk it all on trying to find the big strike, he just sold the stuff everyone else needed to try to find the next big strike themselves.

S&A: How about a few modern examples?

Hunt: Two great "picks and shovels" stories of modern times come from the recent Internet and energy booms: Cisco and Core Laboratories.

Cisco was one of the ultimate "picks and shovels" investment plays of the Internet revolution. Rather than try to pick which website companies were going to be successful, an investor could have just bought Cisco instead.

Cisco made the routers and switches – what some folks called the "plumbing" – required to build the Internet... and the stock climbed more than 9,500% from its IPO in 1992 to the 2000 bubble peak.

Remember... during this time, thousands of companies tried to become the Internet's "next big thing." A handful made it. Most did not. Cisco just sold the "picks and shovels" to build the Internet and soared. It was the surer bet. It was the "sleep at night" bet.

Now, let's take the story of Core Laboratories.

Back in 2003, if investors believed that crude oil was set for a big price rise, they had a handful of different vehicles to choose from. They could buy speculative futures contracts... they could buy a small oil company exploring for oil in some remote jungle... or they could have bought shares in Core Laboratories.

Core Laboratories used specialized technology to analyze oil and gas deposits. They helped oil companies decide where to drill in order to find big deposits and helped them manage those deposits once they were found. Core did no drilling or exploration of its own. It was paid by lots of different market participants who were doing lots of drilling and exploration.

As oil prices climbed from $30 per barrel in 2003 to $100 per barrel in 2008, Core's customers had more money to spend on exploration. Core's revenues surged... and the stock went from $5 per share to $60 per share... a gain of 1,100%.

It was a pure "picks and shovels" play on the oil boom. Rather than take on the risk of owning shares in a company looking for oil in just a handful of places, Core Laboratories investors could sleep soundly. They knew the company was collecting a steady stream of money from a huge number of oil companies.

S&A: Most people don't realize there are "picks and shovels" investments in nearly every industry. Can you give us a few more examples most folks don't realize exist?

Hunt: Sure. I have two more. Let's talk farming, then biotechnology.

In 2006, corn and soybean prices entered a big bull move that took both crops more than 200% higher. Emerging markets like China started growing richer and consuming more livestock... which resulted in increased demand for grain to feed the livestock.

Rather than going out and buying a farm... or going into the futures market to buy corn and soybeans, an investor could have bought shares in fertilizer producers like Potash and Mosaic. These two companies produce and sell the vital fertilizers farmers slather on their fields to increase crop yields.

As crop prices climbed and farm incomes rose, demand for fertilizers increased. Potash shares gained 600% during the boom... Mosaic gained 900%.

Again, we see huge returns were made in companies that sold vital tools, products, and services used by an industry in a big upswing.

Now, developing drugs in the biotechnology field is a lot different from farming, but it has its "picks and shovels" plays as well. For example, there's a type of business called contract research organizations, or CROs.

These are companies that perform lab and testing work for big pharmaceutical and small drug development companies. They assist these companies with the huge undertaking of developing and testing new drugs they hope to one day sell for billions of dollars.

Many drug companies are risky bets on just one or two drugs making it to market. CROs aren't like that. They just do research and development. When the industry is in an upswing, CROs take in revenue from lots of different clients... who are all looking to develop new blockbuster drugs.

From 2003-2008, one of the big CROs, Covance, climbed from $20 per share to $90 per share. It was a way to play the rising tide of the risky biotech sector, with a much surer outcome than buying a company betting it all on one drug.

S&A: Okay... we've covered the rewards of "picks and shovels" ideas. But every investment idea has risks. What are the risks for "picks and shovels"?

Hunt: There are two major risks.

One is company-specific risk. There is a risk the company's managers make bad decisions that reduce their competitive edge. This is where you have to do a great deal of research and know the playing field... or pay a knowledgeable industry expert to do it for you.

I think most folks should stick to the biggest and best players when looking to make "picks and shovels" investments. The larger, more stable companies depend less on debt to conduct business. They have higher profit margins and their cash flows are more stable. Stick with the biggest and best "picks and shovels" companies, and you add another layer of "sleep at night" safety.

The second risk is that when a sector or a commodity booms, it's eventually followed by a bust.

Most "picks and shovels" ideas should not be viewed as long-term investments. They should be viewed more as trades that can last for two, three, even five years.

For example, even the best "picks and shovels" plays in the oil industry will get hammered if oil declines by 50%. Even the best crop fertilizer producers will suffer badly if corn and soybeans enter a long-term bear market. You have to be ready to sell these investments when the market turns.

S&A: Any final words?

Hunt: One last thing... It's important to keep in mind your goals and risk tolerance as an investor.

I'm not attacking the strategy of buying riskier "one shot" exploration or production plays. You can make terrific returns by owning the "one shot" companies. But investing and trading in these types of companies requires more specialized knowledge. They carry more risk... more than most folks are comfortable taking on.

That's why "picks and shovels" can be so useful to the conservative investor.

S&A: Thanks for joining us today.

Hunt: My pleasure.

Summary: When it comes to investing in a big sector or commodity boom, consider the safe, "sleep at night" approach to playing the boom. Consider buying "picks and shovels" companies that supply vital tools, products, and services to the boom's participants.

SHORT SELLING

Most traders and investors attempt to profit from stocks rising in price. "Short sellers" attempt to profit from stocks falling in price.

You'll do just fine by simply avoiding shares of "short candidates." But if you're comfortable taking on a bit of extra risk, short selling the right companies can provide a protective "hedge" for the rest of your portfolio.

The first step, of course, is to know what you're doing. That's why we've interviewed master trader Jeff Clark, editor of the *S&A Short Report*.

If you're looking to profit on the downside, read on...

Stansberry & Associates: Jeff, can you quickly define "short selling" for us?

Jeff Clark: Short selling is the attempt to profit off a decline in stock prices. You're basically selling something you don't own with the expectation you can buy it back later at a lower price.

So it's the opposite of buying low and selling high. With short selling, you sell high first, then buy low later on.

S&A: Many investors have never shorted stocks because they believe it's too difficult or too risky. Why should investors add shorting to their investing skill set?

Clark: Successful investors take advantage of opportunities. It doesn't matter if those opportunities are in the stock market, the bond market, currencies, real estate, whatever. And it shouldn't matter whether those opportunities are on the upside or the downside.

Short selling is an important strategy for any portfolio. Stocks move up *and* down. If you're only investing on the *up* moves, you're only taking advantage of half the opportunities. Shorting is an ideal way to both hedge your portfolio and profit directly from declines in the market.

S&A: Can you briefly explain how to short a stock?

Clark: Technically, the process involves "borrowing" the stock from your brokerage firm (who borrows it from a customer, who owns the shares in a margin account).

For example, if you wanted to short 100 shares of company ABC, you would ask your brokerage firm to borrow 100 shares. If the firm doesn't have any customers with company ABC's stock in a margin account, there wouldn't be any shares available to short and you would not be able to make the trade. If there are shares available, you could sell the shares short. The cash for the sale would then be credited to your account.

I'm going to keep the math basic here, but suppose each share of company ABC is currently trading for $20. Your account would be credited $2,000 for selling those 100 shares short and your position would appear in your account as negative 100 shares of company ABC.

When you decide to close – or "cover" – the position, you would go into the market and buy back 100 shares of company ABC. The negative share balance would be zeroed out, and the purchase price debited from your account.

If your bearish stance was right, and ABC declined 75% to $5 per share, your account would be debited $500... In other words, it would cost you $500 to buy those shares back.

Since it only cost you $5 per share to buy the shares back, you would pocket the difference... in this case $15 per share, or $1,500. That's how a profitable short sale works.

S&A: Are there particular types of stocks that are ideal to short?

Clark: There are three ideal short selling candidates...

First are "fraud" stocks – companies with fake products, deceptive financial statements, snake oil management, etc. These are the toughest to find, but they're usually the most successful short sales.

Look at what happened in 2011 with the Chinese reverse merger companies. You had dozens of companies that took advantage of the hype of the "great China boom." They raised a bunch of money by selling stock to American investors. But the companies weren't viable businesses. Management fabricated the financial statements, announced deals and breakthroughs that never happened, and basically stole investors' money.

China isn't a bad place to find old fashioned, run-of-the-mill, we're-lying-through-our-teeth frauds. But neither is our own backyard. Enron, WorldCom, Bear Stearns, and a whole host of "dotcom" companies... those scandals cost investors billions of dollars. That money is gone... disappeared... evaporated into thin air. The point is, if you're smart enough to recognize the fraud and to capitalize on it, then some of the money, rather than completely vanishing, will find its way into your brokerage account.

Next are companies with flawed business plans. You don't have to look much further than the Internet craze of 2000 to find great examples of bad business plans. These companies didn't intentionally try to deceive investors. They were just never going to show a profit.

When analysts start talking about valuing a company on "page-views" or "eyeballs" or some other screwy method other than profits and earnings, you have to start considering the stock as a short-sale candidate.

Commerce One (CMRC) was probably my most successful short sale back then. Anyone could look at the SEC filings for this business-to-business e-commerce company and figure out it was never, ever going to turn a profit. The numbers simply didn't work out.

Yet, at the peak of the Internet bubble, CMRC was a several-billion-dollar company. I remember selling the stock short at something over $300 per share and then buying it back just a few months later for less than $20.

The third ideal short candidates are overpriced stocks that have broken down technically. It's tough to profitably short stocks only on the basis of valuation. Expensive stocks have a habit of getting more expensive. And as the famous quote goes, "the market can remain irrational longer than you can remain solvent." So timing is important.

EBay is a great example. For years, eBay traded at a valuation that put its price-to-earnings (P/E) ratio above 100. Bulls correctly argued that eBay's high growth rate justified a high P/E multiple. However, at its high point in December 2005, eBay was trading at a whopping 170 times earnings. Its earnings growth rate of 75% justified a high P/E ratio, but 170 was just ridiculous.

The time to sell the stock short was after eBay disclosed that its growth rate was slowing... The announcement dried up the stock's momentum and the share price was nearly cut in half.

S&A: Are there strategies for timing a short sale more successfully?

Clark: Just as it's usually a bad idea to chase a stock's price higher when you're buying, it's also bad to sell short into a rapidly declining market. Stocks that are oversold tend to bounce, sometimes violently. The safest way to sell short is to wait for a stock's momentum to shift from bullish to bearish, especially for the third type of stocks I just mentioned.

One tell-tale sign the momentum has shifted is when the stock price drops below its 50-day moving average (or "DMA").

The 50-DMA is a commonly watched technical level. Generally, when a stock is trading above its 50-DMA, the trend is bullish and traders can use pullbacks in the price to buy into the position. On the other hand, when a stock is trading below the 50-DMA, the trend is bearish and traders can sell short into any rally attempts back up toward the 50-DMA.

So the safest way to short is to look for that break below the 50-DMA... and then wait for the inevitable oversold bounce. If the stock can bounce back up and "kiss" its 50-DMA from below, it's a terrific risk/reward setup for a short trade. The 50-DMA should serve as resistance, and a stock with bearish momentum will have a tough time rallying above that level.

So you'd be shorting at an optimum resistance point and the stock should start trending lower almost immediately. If the stock can somehow rally above the line, it negates the bearish pattern and you can cover the trade for a small loss.

S&A: Besides using moving averages to initiate short positions, are there any other strategies you use to limit risk?

Clark: The best way to manage risk when shorting actually doesn't involve shorting at all.

Nowadays, going through the process of shorting a stock itself is largely unnecessary. Investors can achieve higher returns with less risk by buying put options or creating option combinations.

Any time you buy an option, the most you can lose is the price you pay for that option which is always much less than you would have at risk in the stock. It doesn't require borrowing the stock, and it almost always involves less capital upfront.

So as long as you don't over-leverage the trade, you have a built-in risk management system with options.

The mistake a lot of novice traders make is they take on too large a position. Suppose an investor has the capital available to short sell 100 or 200 shares of a particular stock. In place of short selling those 100 or 200 shares, they'll often buy 10 or 20 put-option contracts.

Since each option contract represents 100 shares of stock, that's like shorting 1,000 or 2,000 shares of stock. It's a much larger position than they would ever take normally. But because options are so cheap relative to the stock, they feel comfortable taking on that sort of leverage, and end up risking much more money than they otherwise would. Inevitably, that excess leverage blows up and the trader suffers a huge loss.

So if you normally trade in 100 or 200 share lots, you should buy one or two put option contracts instead of shorting the stock. If you trade in 1,000 share increments, 10 put contracts give you the same coverage. Don't over-leverage the trade, and the risk will manage itself.

S&A: Is there anything else investors should know about shorting?

Clark: Perhaps the most exciting aspect of short selling is the speed at which profits can occur. Stocks tend to fall a lot faster than they rise. After all, you rarely hear of a "buying panic." So it's not uncommon to earn 30%-50% on a short trade in just a few weeks. If you trade put options, the returns can be considerably larger.

S&A: Thanks for your time, Jeff.

Clark: You're welcome.

Summary: "Short sellers" attempt to profit from stocks falling in price. You'll do just fine simply by avoiding shares of short candidates. But if you're comfortable taking on a bit of extra risk, short selling the right companies can provide a protective "hedge" for the rest of your portfolio.

ANACONDA TRADING

Dr. David Eifrig is the editor of the *Retirement Millionaire* and *Retirement Trader* advisories. As a former professional trader, "Doc" (as we like to call him) is an expert at finding low-risk, high-reward investment opportunities safe enough for even the most risk-averse investor.

Below, Doc shares one of his favorite investment strategies... a "big" idea responsible for some of his most successful trades.

Whether you're just getting started with investing or on the verge of retirement, this idea could dramatically increase your returns while saving you a huge amount of time and money.

Stansberry & Associates: Doc, your advisories – *Retirement Millionaire* and *Retirement Trader* – are centered around an idea you call "anaconda trading." Can you define this idea for us?

Dr. David Eifrig: Sure... First, "anaconda trading" doesn't pertain to a particular trading strategy. Instead, it's a framework to think about trading and investing. It's how many of the world's richest and most successful investors grow and protect their wealth.

I realize it might seem like a silly comparison, but I've found the most useful way to describe this approach is in terms of the anaconda. Anacondas are the largest snakes in the world. And they're one of the deadliest, most efficient predators... but they don't hunt like most other animals.

Anacondas don't "zip" around chasing after their prey. They don't get into long battles with them. In fact, they don't hunt in a traditional sense at all.

Instead, they lie around in rivers for long periods of time. They wait for an unsuspecting animal to pass by or stop for a drink of water. Only then do they strike... by slowly wrapping themselves around the prey and holding on until the animal stops breathing. Then, with their large mouth, they swallow their prey whole. It's a unique strategy in nature. They're nature's "cheap shot" artists.

Said another way, anacondas aren't interested in fair fights... They'll only strike when the odds are overwhelmingly on their side. They're "no risk" operators. And they take their time waiting for their prey and, once it's captured, waiting for the capture to pay off.

Anacondas can grow to enormous size because they don't spend much time or energy chasing every animal that comes along.

S&A: How do you apply this idea to investing?

Eifrig: Well, that's how the world's best investors think about buying stocks, bonds, and commodities. They act only when the odds are heavily stacked in their favor. In a similar way, their portfolios can grow to enormous size because they're greatly reducing risk.

If you begin to think about investing this way, you can avoid a huge amount of worry and wasted time, and set yourself up to make extraordinary returns. Like the anaconda, you can rest along the river bank until the right opportunity presents itself.

S&A: Can you give us an example of how you've used this approach?

Eifrig: Sure, a great example was in 2010 when bank analyst Meredith Whitney went on *60 Minutes* and predicted hundreds of billions of dollars of losses in the municipal bond market. Muni bonds collapsed in price, but I thought it was a major overreaction... the predictions were factually incorrect. So we were able to buy these bonds at a major discount with little risk, simply by waiting for a fantastic opportunity to come to us. And we made great, safe returns over the next several years.

S&A: How about an example of how this idea applies to shorter-term trading?

Eifrig: One of my favorite ways to use this idea for trading is to take advantage of spikes in volatility. The Volatility Index, also known as the "VIX" or "fear index," tends to rise as stocks fall and investors become more fearful.

The VIX is also used to determine option prices... When volatility spikes, options become more expensive. Yet these periods of high volatility typically don't last long... and as any professional trader will tell you, most options expire worthless.

So when we occasionally see a big spike in volatility, it often makes sense to sell – essentially short-sell – puts on stocks you'd like to own anyway. The ins and outs of selling puts are beyond the scope of this interview, but this is an ideal "anaconda" situation.

One of the best examples of this is the stock crash of late 2008 and early 2009. Investors who were patient and prudent were able to collect a huge amount of low-risk income, and pick up some of the world's best companies at absurdly cheap prices.

S&A: Are there any risks or hurdles with "anaconda trading"?

Eifrig: Because it's a framework rather than a specific strategy, there aren't really risks in the traditional sense. Followed prudently, it can only help you. It's a simple idea, but it can be quite difficult for the novice investor to apply consistently. You'll learn patience and discipline.

Few people are naturally wired with the patience required to be successful investors. In fact, it's often just the opposite. Many investors act as though frequent buying and selling is the ticket to huge wealth. But it's exactly this behavior that ensures the average investor will never build real wealth through investing.

It doesn't help that Wall Street does all it can to encourage this behavior – that's where the commissions are made – and the financial media are constantly talking about the latest hot stock picks.

For most people, this is something they have to work at... a skill they have to build. But it's one of the best things you can do to improve your investing and trading results immediately. I recommend everyone give it a try.

S&A: Thanks for talking with us, Doc.

Eifrig: You're welcome.

Summary: "Anaconda trading" is all about patience... developing the patience to hold cash and savings and sit tight until the ideal opportunity presents itself... an opportunity where the odds are overwhelmingly stacked in your favor, and the risk of loss is dramatically reduced.

SELLING PUTS

According to Stansberry & Associates founder Porter Stansberry, most people will probably never get involved in options...

You have to do what you're comfortable with... and do what you understand. "But know this," he continues, "You can make 5% or more every few months, nearly risk-free, in the options markets. You do this by selling options, not buying them."

Buying options can be incredibly risky. As Porter explains, "It's a strategy that should be used mostly by professional investors to hedge against losses – insurance, essentially. Buying options is a cost of doing business for professional fund managers. Selling those options is an easy way for us to generate large amounts of safe income."

How safe is selling options? To discuss this idea, we sat down with Dr. David Eifrig, who has been showing readers of his *Retirement Trader* advisory how to use options to generate safe income.

To learn more about this radical approach to generating income, read on...

Stansberry & Associates: Doc, you've told folks looking for a conservative, high-income, retirement-friendly trading strategy they can't find a better tool than selling put options. Can you explain how this strategy works?

Dr. David Eifrig: Sure. Put options work the same way as homeowners insurance. When you insure your home, you are simply buying the right to sell your house to the insurance company if certain things happen, like a fire or a storm.

In return for that protection, you pay the insurance company a certain fee – known as the insurance premium – to accept those terms, whether or not you ever actually exercise the insurance policy. And most homes don't burn down... Most homes don't blow away in a storm.

With put options, instead of buying the protection, you're acting like the insurance company.

You see, when you sell a put option, you're agreeing to buy someone else's stock at a certain price – known as the "strike" price – under certain conditions, for a limited period of time. In return, you're getting paid a certain fee – the option premium – to accept those terms.

In the example of home insurance, a person would exercise the policy only after a catastrophic event... when something like a fire or severe weather damages the value of his or her home.

Again, a put option works the same way. In this case, the holder would exercise his right to sell the stock to you only if the market value of the stock falls below the strike price you agreed to pay.

If the stock goes up or even stays where it is – as long as it doesn't fall below the strike price – you get to keep your premium. If it does drop below that price, you're obligated to buy the stock, but the premium you received ensures you get a discount to the current price. It's almost like being paid to buy a stock at a discount – or getting paid to offer $250,000 for a house the buyer is asking $300,000 for.

And the best part of the strategy is you don't have to be right forever. You just need to be right for a few months, because your obligation to buy expires when the option expires.

S&A: Can you walk us through an example with a stock?

Eifrig: One of my favorite examples is Johnson & Johnson (JNJ). It's a big, strong company, it pays a growing dividend, and it stands to benefit from one of the biggest trends in the world: the increased medical spending of aging Baby Boomers.

In early 2011, the company announced some product recalls that caused the shares to sell off a bit. But the company had moved to correct the problems, so I thought the selling was overdone... And the company had just released a great earnings report. So shares were cheaper, but all the great points I mentioned earlier were still intact.

So we took advantage in *Retirement Trader* and sold puts on JNJ. Like all put-selling trades, there were two potential outcomes here. If the stock stayed at our strike price or moved higher, we would get to keep our premium and make a quick 8% gain in just three months. This works out to an annualized return of 30%-40%. On the other hand, if the stock fell below our strike price, we'd own the shares at a discount to the even cheaper price.

When you're talking about a quality company like JNJ, that is a win-win proposition.

S&A: But what happens if the stock crashes, say because of an accounting scandal or a major product recall?

Eifrig: In that scenario, you would have to buy a stock for much more than it is currently trading for. It could happen because every investment carries risk, and no one can predict the future.

So, one key to selling puts safely is figuring out what the company's stock is really worth and trading the best companies.

Just like an insurance company needs to know the details of your home – things like how much you paid for it, how big it is, the value of any valuables you have, and so on – you need to know the details of the companies you sell puts on to be sure they're fundamentally sound.

An insurance company wouldn't want to insure an old house with a faulty electrical system. Similarly, you don't want to "insure" just any stock. You want to find quality stocks that you like and would want to own anyway. Then, you "insure" them – sell puts on them – at a price they aren't likely to drop below.

Since you're only agreeing to buy the stock below the strike price, you're safe as long as it doesn't completely crash. Again, this is why you want to stick with quality companies.

When this strategy is used correctly, you won't end up buying very many stocks... You'll simply collect premiums every few months and earn 15% a year or more on your capital.

But it's no problem if you do end up buying a few stocks. If you follow a few simple rules, you'll own some great dividend-paying companies at great prices that will compound your wealth for years.

S&A: You've made a convincing case for selling put options. Any closing thoughts?

Eifrig: No other strategy offers a chance to safely profit, no matter what happens to stock prices. I truly believe it's one of the most valuable investing skills you can learn.

Contrary to popular opinion, I think it's within reach of any serious investor. It does require some education for most folks to become proficient, but there are a number of free resources available out there. The time and effort you spend learning will be well worth it.

Of course, I invite folks to take a look at my *Retirement Trader* advisory as well. Our goal is not only to find the safest and most profitable trades, but to educate. In fact, if most subscribers don't eventually become proficient at finding and making these trades for themselves, I'm not doing my job.

S&A: Thanks for talking with us, Doc.

Eifrig: My pleasure. Thanks for inviting me.

Summary: Selling puts is a simple way to generate income and potentially "buy" the stocks you want to own, at the exact price you want to pay, while minimizing risk and greatly increasing potential returns.

SELLING COVERED CALLS

S&A Short Report editor and master trader Jeff Clark calls this idea "the single best income generating strategy ever created."

It's known as "covered-call writing," and Jeff has used it to make a fortune for himself and his readers over the years.

To learn more about this low-risk way to earn more income from your investments, keep reading...

Stansberry & Associates: Jeff, could you explain how covered-call writing can dramatically increase the amount of income you receive from your investments?

Jeff Clark: Sure. "Covered-call writing," which is sometimes referred to as "selling covered calls," is my favorite strategy to generate investment income from a portfolio.

I had a client once who started out with 2,000 shares of a company called Siebel Systems. By using this strategy, we were able to generate an incredible half-million dollars in income in just a single year. The guy bought a vacation home in Tahoe with his earnings.

In a nutshell, the strategy involves buying a stock, and then selling someone else a contract that gives them the right to buy that stock from you at a predetermined time in the future. These types of contracts are called "options."

S&A: When putting this idea into context for folks in the past, you explained it in terms of buying and selling real estate. Can you go into that idea here?

Clark: Let's say you buy a piece of property for $200,000. You then turn around and sell someone the right to buy it from you any time in the next three months for $210,000. For that right, you charge a fee of, say, 4%, or $8,000.

You pocket the $8,000 immediately. It's your money now. You are also obliged to sell the property for $210,000 if the buyer chooses to exercise his right.

This scenario has three possible outcomes...

First, the property goes up in value, and the buyer exercises his right to buy. In this case, you've pocketed the $8,000 premium, and you'll be selling the property for $210,000. Here, you'll have an $18,000 gain (9%) in three months, and you'll have to find another investment property to buy in order to continue the strategy.

Second, the property remains worth $200,000. In this case, you keep the $8,000 premium. Since the buyer won't be willing to pay $210,000 for a property that's only worth $200,000, you'll keep the property, too. You've made 4% over three months, and you can even sell the right to buy your property again, presumably for another $8,000!

Third, the property falls in value. In this case, the $8,000 premium you received helps to offset the loss on the property. The buyer walks away when the right expires, and you're also free to sell another right.

So if the investment goes up, then we sell it for a gain. If the investment stays the same, then we profit off the premium. And if the investment drops in value, then the premium helps offset the loss.

S&A: Now how about a hypothetical example with a stock?

Clark: Let's say you buy shares of stock ABC at $20 per share. You think it's a great value at $20.

You can sell someone the right to buy your shares from you at $22 per share. You receive $1 per share for agreeing to sell your stock at a higher price. And the contract is good for three months.

If ABC rises to $23 in three months, you have to honor your agreement and sell your stock for $22 per share. You collect $2 in capital gains, and you keep the $1 per share you received for entering the contract. In this case, you make $3 per share on your purchase price of $20 per share. That's a return of 15% in three months, which is fantastic.

S&A: What happens if ABC does not rise in price? What if it trades sideways for the next three months?

Clark: You do nothing. You just keep that $1 per share you received for entering the contract. That payment – which is called a "premium" – is yours to keep, no matter what happens. That's a 5% return on your stock position. In the case of ABC trading sideways over the next three months, you'd keep the premium and possibly look to do the same transaction again.

S&A: Great. You make money if ABC goes up, and you make money if ABC trades sideways. What if ABC goes down?

Clark: If ABC goes down, the $1 you received for entering the contract cushions your loss. And since you think ABC is a great value, you'd probably hold onto it and look to sell more calls against your position.

S&A: It sounds like a terrific strategy. Are there any pitfalls?

Clark: There are two major pitfalls...

First of all, if the investment collapses, the small premium you received by selling the option won't do much to alleviate the loss on your "safe" money. If a stock drops a little, say 10%-20%, you can make up for some of the loss by selling the premium a few times. But you will not be safe from a 50% loss with this strategy.

With this strategy, you want to look for low-risk stocks where the options can generate 15%-20% annual returns.

The other pitfall to covered-call writing is that you sell off your potential for enormous gains.

Take our real estate example. We are obligated to sell the property for $210,000. That's a good gain, especially considering the extra $8,000 premium. But if the property jumps to $300,000, then we'll be kicking ourselves for selling at such a cheap price.

But here's the thing... The purpose of covered-call writing is to generate income, not capital gains. It's the difference between buying a bond and buying a stock. Stock buyers look for capital gains. Income is secondary. Bond buyers want the income, and any gains are a bonus. Folks who write covered calls are similar to bond buyers.

If you like the prospects of a stock and believe it could easily double or triple, then don't sell options against it. You'd cap your profit potential and guarantee that you'll be out of the trade before it goes higher.

To put it another way, you should only sell calls against stocks that you wouldn't mind selling at the agreed upon price.

S&A: This is where many folks go wrong with a covered call strategy, right?

Clark: Yes.

Although it involves the use of options, covered-call writing is really quite safe and simple. But many people think this is a risky strategy... because most people do it wrong.

They buy high-risk stocks because the option premiums are expensive and generate the largest current return. But then, the stocks collapse, and investors are stuck with losses.

The secret here is to focus on not losing money by buying low-risk value stocks and then selling the calls. If you do that, then the returns come quite easily. That's it.

I keep the risk very low by picking the right stocks. By focusing on conservative, value-oriented stocks, we eliminate a lot of the volatility that can wipe out several months' worth of gains overnight. We also avoid the temptation to chase the highest-yielding covered-call positions, as those tend to be the trades that are most likely to blow-up.

Understand that this is different than the way in which most people approach covered-call writing. Most people start by looking for options that carry the fattest premium and then find a way to justify owning the stock. That's why most people have a tough time generating consistent income through covered-call writing.

S&A: Thanks for talking with us today.

Clark: Thank you.

Summary: "Covered-call writing" can dramatically increase the amount of income you receive from your investments. It involves buying a stock, and then selling someone else an options contract that gives them the right to buy that stock from you at a predetermined time in the future. Only sell covered calls on safe, cheap stocks.

ALTERNATIVE INVESTMENTS

RESOURCE "HOARDING"

In this interview, master resource investor Rick Rule discusses one of the most powerful strategies for profiting in natural resources...

Rick has spent decades in the resource markets, making himself and his clients a fortune in the process. He has also financed several of the most important resource companies in the world. No one is more qualified to explain this idea.

What you'll read below is not complicated, but don't let that fool you. Rick has personally used this idea to make mind-boggling amounts of money in resource stocks.

If you're looking to do the same, read on...

Stansberry & Associates: Rick, of all the ways to invest in resources, the strategy of "hoarding" may be the simplest... But it can also be extremely profitable – and relatively safe – when done correctly. Before we get into how this idea works, can you define what hoarding is?

Rick Rule: Sure. Hoarding is simply buying resources in the ground and holding them, rather than mining or extracting them. Companies that do this are known as "hoarders."

S&A: What is the benefit of hoarding?

Rule: To fully appreciate the beauty of the strategy, you must first understand a fact about the mining business: It's a *terrible* business.

It's a business where your asset base – the resources in the mine – is declining consistently over time, you have huge capital costs for building the mines and maintaining expensive equipment, and you're often exposed to huge political risks because you can't just pack up a mine and move it. On top of all that, many mining executives are less than shareholder-friendly.

So when you buy a mining stock, you must understand that is the business you're buying into.

Now imagine if you could get many of the positives of owning the resources in a mine, but without the negatives associated with mining. That is the benefit of hoarding.

Hoarders accumulate mines and undeveloped resource deposits, and basically just sit on them. Because they don't operate mines, they don't have the huge capital costs and risks of traditional mining companies.

Their share price is simply a leveraged play on the price of the underlying resource. When prices rise, the value of the company's deposits increase as well.

S&A: You've been intimately involved with this strategy... Can you give us some examples of how profitable it can be?

Rule: Certainly. During the bear market in resources during the 1990s and early 2000s, we were able to employ this strategy with great success.

At the time, there was no constituency for resource stocks at all. A group of us in the business came to the realization that exploring for things like heavy oil, natural gas, copper, uranium, and even gold and silver made no sense at the time. But we could buy the successful efforts of prior explorers – where the deposits weren't profitable at the then-prevailing prices – often for pennies on the dollar. Because we believed that commodity prices had nowhere to go but up, this made perfect sense.

As an example, during that time we financed Silver Standard – one of the world's biggest owners of silver mines – at $0.72 a share, or about $2 million. But instead of mining the deposits, we just held them. As other proven mines became available, we bought them, too. When silver soared in the bull market of the 2000s, it became a $1 billion-plus company.

Another great example was Paladin Resources, a uranium hoarder.

It was buying uranium when absolutely nobody cared about it. We bought it at $0.10 a share, and I remember selling some of that stock at $10 a share.

As you can see, the leverage these companies can provide to rising commodity prices is just incredible.

S&A: What are the guidelines for hoarding stocks?

Rule: The ideal time to buy these stocks is at the bottom of a resource cycle or during times of great pessimism. When the price of a particular commodity is low, mining companies in the sector can't produce a profit, and most investors are completely uninterested.

It's at these times when the hoarder stocks are at their cheapest, safest, and most attractive. Take uranium after the Fukushima disaster as a great example.

Of course, because hoarders are so leveraged to the price of the underlying resource, they can be a good speculation on rising prices and a hedge against inflation. Just remember that leverage is a double-edged sword, so the volatility will typically be much greater than that of the actual commodity.

I should also mention that successfully owning these stocks requires a great deal of discipline and patience. These stocks can return hundreds and hundreds of times your money, but they often require several years to do so.

Are you prepared to wait five, 10, or more years for those kinds of returns? Most investors would impulsively say yes, but in practice, many have trouble holding a stock for 10 weeks, never mind 10 years. People want immediate gratification. But in my experience, immediate gratification is very seldom on offer in the financial markets.

S&A: That's a great point... Are there any significant risks to owning these stocks?

Rule: Because they aren't involved in the mining business, these stocks are generally less risky than the miners... But there are still some risks.

While they don't have to pay the huge capital costs of mining, they do still have to pay for expenses like property taxes, fees, and overhead. They don't mine, so they're typically cash flow negative. This means they can get into trouble and be extraordinarily volatile during times when access to capital becomes difficult. You must be prepared for that.

Also, because these company's resource estimates are usually based on drilling and assays rather than actual production, the stocks trade at a significant discount to active mining companies. This isn't necessarily a risk, but it's another good reason to concentrate your purchases at times of great pessimism.

As I frequently say, you have to be a contrarian or you will be a victim.

S&A: Thanks for the insight, Rick.

Rule: My pleasure. Thanks for having me.

Summary: The best time to buy "hoarder" stocks is at the bottom of a resource cycle or during times of great pessimism. Because they are so leveraged to the price of the underlying resource, they can be a good speculation on rising prices and a hedge against inflation.

THE CONSERVATIVE, COMMON SENSE WAY TO INVEST IN RENTAL REAL ESTATE

Investing in real estate is a time-tested way for regular people to build large fortunes. Almost everyone has a friend or family member who has made great money with a rental property.

However, it's very easy to go wrong in real estate. Some people take an amateur approach. Some take a professional's common sense, conservative approach.

To learn why the latter approach is best, read the following interview with professional real estate investor Justin Ford. It's a quick read... and could help you safely make hundreds of thousands – even millions – of dollars in real estate.

Stansberry & Associates: Justin... buying rental real estate is a time-tested way to preserve and grow wealth. But people can go very wrong in real estate if they focus on the wrong things. You've developed a great, common sense way to invest in real estate. Could you describe this approach?

Justin Ford: Sure.

There's an acronym I use to tell people what I think the four most important aspects of real estate are. The acronym is CAPA. It stands for cash flow, amortization, positive leverage, and appreciation.

The first three you can control. You can control whether you buy a property that has cash flow or not, whether you put a loan on it that amortizes or not, and whether that loan has positive leverage or not.

The only thing you can't control is the fourth item, which is appreciation. Unfortunately, that's the one thing that everyone focuses on. Everyone plays appreciation as if it were a point-and-click game in the stock market. It's not. And that's why many people got into trouble during the housing bust.

The good news is, if you focus on the first three things – cash flow, amortization, and positive leverage – you can almost guarantee a positive return.

A lot of things would have to go wrong for you not to be successful. You'd have to have a lot of bad luck or you'd have to be a very bad practitioner, one or the other, or a combination of the two.

But if you're a moderately successful practitioner with just average luck and you focus on those three things, you should have a positive outcome. And the sharper you are as a practitioner, the better the outcome.

S&A: Let's cover cash flow first. Could you walk us through the numbers to keep in mind when computing cash flow for a potential investment?

Ford: Absolutely. Positive cash flow is just like anything else in any business you run. You have to make enough money to pay your expenses, and then you have to have a little left over for the unexpected. Whether it's a Laundromat, a dog kennel, or a candy store, cash flow is king. It's the same thing with property.

Now, people don't think of it that way with property because many new investors in real estate have been conditioned to invest in the stock market. They're not really prepared. They're just trained to invest the way brokers want them to invest, which is point-and-click, buy, sell, buy, sell. It's all price driven.

S&A: Most people in the stock market are obsessed with capital appreciation. They want to double their money on some hot growth stock rather than focusing on cash flow and income from dividends.

Ford: Right. And here's the proof. If I ask the average stock investor "Do you own Google?" and they say yes, then I'll ask, "Well, how much did Google earn last year and how much did it earn this year?"

They won't know Google's cash flow. But if you ask them what the shares are trading for, they'll know the answer. That's because they are focused on share price and share price appreciation... and not much else.

Of course, if you're involved in the day-to-day operation of a business or a property, then you're focusing on cash flow. Whether it's a house, an apartment building, a mobile-home park, or an office building, cash flow is king. Your cash flow must at least pay your expenses.

Let's take a $100,000 property as an example. We'll imagine it's a house and $100,000 is your investment. And let's say that that property produces $20,000 a year in gross potential income, meaning every month you can rent it out for around $1,600. By the end of the year, you receive around $20,000 if your property is rented out every month.

Now, things never go perfectly, so you're going to have some vacancies. You're going to have this, that, and the other happen. You'll also have normal expenses – things like real estate taxes, insurance, maintenance, repairs, minor things like license fees, maybe accounting fees, and if you're not managing it yourself you'll have a management fee, etc.

It's not unusual for about 50% of a property's gross income to go towards expenses. Let's say of this $20,000, $10,000 is consumed by expenses, vacancy, and collection losses. That means you're left over with $10,000 as net operating income. That's a really good deal. You spent $100,000 and you got $10,000 back that you can theoretically put in your pocket, so that's a 10% return.

Now, being a prudent investor you're not going to put all $10,000 in your pocket. You're going to keep $2,000-$4,000 – depending on what you foresee in the future – as reserves. But still that $10,000 right now belongs to you. It's your net operating income. And that's a good return. That's cash flow.

Now, let me tell you what happened in the bubble (2003-2007). In the bubble, people didn't do cash flow. They would buy some ridiculous $400,000 home that used to sell for $150,000, and they were hoping to sell it for $500,000. And the rents on that thing were maybe $15,000 to $20,000 a year. They weren't even good operators, so they wouldn't get the $15,000 or $20,000. They might only get $10,000 in rent out of that house.

And then all of a sudden that house that used to be worth $150,000 is now worth $400,000. The taxes have gone up, the insurance has gone up. So now the $10,000 they're squeezing out of there on the rents while they're hoping to flip it doesn't even pay their bills. It doesn't pay their maintenance, their repairs, their license, their accounting, their advertising. It doesn't pay a lot of things. So they're negative.

So they're coming out of pocket, but it's OK. They still think, "It's only a few grand and we all know real estate goes up forever, so who cares?" They "know" they can sell it for $500,000. And they do it once or twice and it works, and they're geniuses.

But then once it all stops, you have nothing but cash flow going out, not coming in. We all know what happens then: The value of the property goes down. They may have loans on it, so now they owe more than the house, and they're hurting. And then they end up with their credit destroyed. They lose all the properties they had.

The moral of the story: If you focus on cash flow – even if you're a flipper, even if you like to buy and sell and never want to be a landlord – flip cash flow. Flip cash flow properties. Don't flip non-cash flow properties. If your flip "flops" you want to have a Plan B.

If your flip doesn't work out – if the market peaks, if some disaster happens and all of a sudden the market becomes scared and no one buys anything – you're OK. You'll be able to bide your time and break even. I have a few properties that went underwater, that are worth less than the loans on them. But they all produce cash flow, and so they carried themselves through that tough time.

S&A: Okay... how about the first "A" in CAPA?

Ford: The "A" of CAPA stands for amortization.

Amortization is basically the gradual, steady reduction of the loan balance. That's all it is.

It comes from the Latin *mors*, meaning "death." So basically, I think about killing off the debt. If you borrow $100,000 at 6%, your monthly payment's going to be $600.

At the very beginning of the loan, $500 and change of that will be interest and the rest will be principal, slightly reducing it. Because you're only charged interest on the principal, as the principal goes down the interest on your next payment is less. But the payment is always $600. So in the beginning of the loan, maybe $540 or so is interest and $60 is principal. Ten years later, maybe $450 is interest, $150 is principal. Ten years after that it might be half and half. And then, the last five years or so, the thing might be 80% principal and 20% interest.

It seems like few people really understand the power of amortization. Of the people flipping real estate and so forth, most of them aren't even familiar with what the term means. And it's a shame because it's the slowest but surest form of wealth growth.

If you buy a $100,000 property with $20,000 down and you put an amortizing loan on it for 30 years... 30 years later the balance will be zero. Your tenants will have paid it off. And in effect, you will have turned $20,000 into $100,000 in 30 years' time, basically guaranteed – assuming you're operating as you expect it to operate.

And that's not assuming any appreciation. With zero appreciation you turn $20,000 into $100,000. Let's say you use a little more leverage and just put $10,000 down. Now you're turning $10,000 into $100,000, with zero appreciation. How powerful is that?

I mean, look at your retirement plan. You're young. 30 years from now, any property you bought for 20% down is going to be worth 100%, assuming *zero* appreciation.

And if you do have appreciation, you turn $20,000 into $200,000 or $300,000. So that's the power of amortization, reducing the loan balance as you go along. Whenever you have that opportunity, you should take advantage of it.

S&A: OK, is there anything else we should touch on with amortization?

Ford: Just that the gains that come from amortization are essentially tax free. You get the tax-free benefit of having someone else pay off your loan.

S&A: Let's move onto the "P" in CAPA.

Ford: The "P" in the CAPA acronym stands for positive leverage.

This is basically where the cost of your borrowing money is less than your cash flow and it's going to stay that way because you fix your interest rate. Put simply, the cost of your debt is less than your cash flow.

So let's go back to that $100,000 property. It generates $20,000 per year in revenue and there's $10,000 in expenses, so you have $10,000 in net operating income. If you're an all-cash buyer, meaning you're making 10% annually, that's your cash yield.

Now if you put a loan on it, you're going to increase your total expenses because you're going to have an interest expense, but you're going to decrease the amount of capital you outlay – the borrowing money. And that return, when using positive leverage, is going to go up. So instead of 10% you might end up with 22% in yield per year.

So let's see how it works. Let's say you're borrowing $80,000 at 5.5% percent. Well, your payments every year, including principal and interest, are going to be roughly around $5,600 And that's going to be paid from that $10,000 cash flow that we talked about, right?

So now, you're left over with $4,400. But instead of putting $100,000 in, you only put in $20,000. So $4,400 divided by $20,000 is 22%. So your cash-on-cash yield went up from 10% to 22%.

Now, let's imagine you get lucky and the property goes up 10% in the first two years you own it – not far from the long-term average. In the first case, where you were an all-cash buyer, that 10% rise was a 10% return on your capital.

With no positive leverage, you put $100,000 in, and you made an extra 10%. In the second case scenario, you made an extra 50%, because it's $10,000 on the $20,000 that you put down. That's the power of positive leverage. In this case, you made 22% two years in a row. And then you made 50% on your amortization. You made 94% gross – we're not doing taxes or anything else right now; we're just talking gross numbers – because you had positive leverage working that property. If you were an all-cash buyer, you would've made 30%. You still would've made a decent return, but not a great return. That's positive leverage.

What's negative leverage? Negative leverage is when you borrow money and you have $10,000 in net operating income – the same example – but your cost of money is $15,000. In this case, you have to come out of pocket just to pay it.

Back in the boom years, no one cared about negative leverage because they "knew" that they would be able to flip for a higher price. The moment that stopped being true, they were stuck with the negative leverage. And then when they tried to sell the property, the property was worth less than before. So not only did they have negative cash flow, they had negative equity. And eventually, they lost their credit and everything else.

So one of the takeaways here: Fix your interest rate so you have positive leverage for as long as you can. I have loans from 2003/2004 that were 6% loans that are fixed for 30 years, and they're just working away. They're chipping away at their payoff date. A lot of these properties still have good, positive equity, and some are a little less than that. But they're all fixed. And that's the conservative route.

S&A: Terrific. And now we should move on to...

Ford: Appreciation.

S&A: Yes, the last "A" of your CAPA acronym. I have a feeling this will be the shortest discussion, because the other three are the most important, correct?

Ford: That's correct. Appreciation is what can make you the richest, combined with positive leverage. But it's the one that you have no control over, and so it's the one that you should not focus on.

However, it's the one that most people focus on. And that's a shame because they neglected all the things they can control. They shoot for the thing they can't, and then they get hammered. But if you get appreciation in addition to those three things we talked about – cash flow, amortization, and positive leverage – you should do well.

If you get appreciation to boot, you could do extremely well – in investor terms, you could do 20%, 30%, 40%, 50% annual returns in many cases when you're getting appreciation combined with those other factors. Long term, you're not going to get that. But long term, you could certainly get 20% returns per year compounded, if you're getting appreciation combined with everything else.

But don't hang your hat on appreciation. Go into everything you buy where if it never appreciated by a dollar you'd still be OK. There are many properties I buy today where I have every reason to believe that they will probably appreciate. For instance, they're selling at less than the cost of replacement value.

If they gave you the land for free, you still couldn't build it at the cost you're buying it. The cost to own is now much cheaper than the cost to rent. So eventually that will create buying pressure because people will stop renting and they'll move to buying and they'll create demand for the actual property.

And then of course, there is the whole inflationary scenario. When you talk about the prospect of inflation, housing is one of the most sensitive inflation indicators in the economy. Much of what the inflation index is made of is in housing – concrete and lumber and steel and labor and tar and petroleum products. And it's almost impossible to imagine those things going up without housing going up.

If we do have appreciation, we'll do extremely well. But if for some reason appreciation goes nowhere and we stay flat, you can still do well. If for some reason, we go nowhere and we go into some great depression of demand and our prices continue to fall and stay low for a long time, you could still do well with the first three things we talked about. You could still make a positive cash flow and have your loan paid off. Obviously, it's not the best scenario. But that to me is smart investing, focusing on those three things.

Summary: When it comes to investing in rental real estate, the concepts of cash flow, amortization, and positive leverage are your best friends. Use them to conservatively build wealth with rental real estate. These are the aspects of real estate investment that you can control. If you get price appreciation (the part you can't control), it's gravy.

HOW TO MAKE THE BIGGEST, SAFEST RETURNS POSSIBLE IN ROYALTY COMPANIES

The interview below features one of the best precious-metals investments in the world: royalty companies.

To explain the incredible benefits of these stocks, we sat down with John Doody, one of the world's top experts on gold and silver stocks.

John is the editor of *Gold Stock Analyst*, an advisory with a track record that's unrivaled in the newsletter industry. John has been studying and analyzing these stocks for over 40 years. And his recommended portfolio averaged returns of 35% per year from 2000 through 2012.

His opinion on gold stocks is so respected, he's been profiled by *Barron's* seven times, quoted in *The Financial Times*, and is frequently interviewed on CNBC. He counts several of the world's best-known gold funds and investment managers among his subscribers. As our colleague Porter Stansberry says, "No one in the world knows more about gold- and silver-producing companies than John Doody. No one else even comes close."

Whether you're just getting started in resource stock investing or you already own some of these companies, John's advice could be critical to making the biggest, safest returns possible in this volatile sector.

Stansberry & Associates: John, you're one of the world's top experts on gold and silver stocks. And follow several "royalty companies." Before we get into the value of owning these stocks, can you define what a royalty company is?

John Doody: A royalty company is basically a mine-financing entity that has sold shares to the public. These companies provide money to miners for either exploration or actual capital costs such as mine and processing-plant construction. So in a sense, they compete with bank lenders and equity offerings that brokers want to do for mining companies.

Royalty companies provide this financing to mining companies in exchange for one of two types of future payments. In the first type, the royalty company will finance an exploration program to receive a royalty on any future sales that are produced from any discovery – which is kind of like a sales tax – that typically ranges from 1%-5% of sales. While the upfront money can be small – often just a few million dollars – the royalties can be quite big. One royalty company we like steadily receives about $50 million per year from a site it helped fund exploration for in the mid-1980s.

In the second type, the royalty company will help finance mine construction – which is much more expensive than funding an exploration program – and receive a royalty payment called a "stream." A stream is a commitment for either a certain number of ounces of metals per year or a certain percentage of ounces produced on an annual basis from the mine.

In this second type, a royalty company might be able to buy streams of gold at a 75% discount to the current spot price. But in order to buy gold at that kind of discount, it has to put up a significant amount of capital upfront.

Streams are often the preferred financing methods for the mining companies. If they borrow the money from a bank, they might have to hedge the production... or the bank might want more security of other mining assets, and so forth. If they sell more shares to finance the mine, it dilutes – and irritates – existing stockholders. So it's generally an easier financing mechanism for the miners, and it's a nice stream of income that the royalty company earns over the life of the mine.

S&A: What makes royalty companies such great investments?

Doody: First, it's a great way to get diversification.

From an investor's standpoint, the typical mature royalty company has a portfolio of anywhere from 10 or 15 up to 50 different mines that are paying them royalties and streams.

So it's a broad, diversified portfolio compared to a typical mining company that might own one or two mines. And as you know, there's a lot of risk associated with a one- or two-mine company. It's common to see mines encounter difficulties for various reasons, and the related mining stocks might lose 25%, 50%, or more of their value in one day.

On the other hand, if a big royalty company had a royalty on that mine, it wouldn't be a big deal, because there would be royalties from other mines that could take up the slack.

You also have a degree of transparency and clarity you don't get with mining stocks. Royalty pipelines are typically pretty visible, particularly over a three- or four-year time frame. And once a royalty company has put the money in, it doesn't have any further risk.

If there are capital cost overruns – and that can be a big problem for mines because they often cost more to build than what was planned – they're not the royalty company's problem. It's already struck its deal. It might take another bite of it, but that would be a new deal. It's not something that the royalty comany would have to pay any portion of. The miner is responsible for all overruns in the construction budget.

There's also no exposure to the rising costs of production that miners have. The production cost of an ounce of gold or silver has gone up dramatically over time. For example, the average cost of production for an ounce of gold in the early 2000s was around $200 an ounce. By 2012, the average cost to produce an ounce of gold was close to $650... and it's only likely to go higher.

A third benefit of royalty companies is they typically pay higher dividends than even some of the biggest mining companies. They have very low overhead. I don't think any of the big ones have more than 20 employees, because you don't need a lot of people in the business. And that means that a very high percentage of royalty income – typically over 90% – goes to gross profits, and from this they pay dividends and taxes, and finance future royalties and streams.

Usually, they pay out about 20% of their royalty income as a dividend, which gives you great current income and visible growth from the royalty pipeline.

S&A: Based on those traits – diversification, relative safety, and high dividends – some folks might assume these stocks don't experience big growth. Is that true?

Doody: No, not really. Royalty companies typically provide strong, steady growth... and much less risky growth, in my opinion.

One of the disadvantages of these companies is there's a lot of unfamiliarity about them among investors. They don't really understand the unique features that make them much more predictable in terms of their growth and their dividends. I think as their pluses get more widely known, their stock prices will react higher.

S&A: Can you provide a couple of examples of how royalty companies can grow to the sky?

Doody: One of the best-known royalty companies is Royal Gold. It's a great example of a royalty company that started small and steadily grew to a multibillion-dollar business.

Royal Gold had the original idea of exploring to grow its own properties, and then finding majors to develop them, while retaining a royalty interest in them.

The company had explored and found gold on a property in Nevada called Cortez. It got a miner called Placer Dome to develop it, and Royal Gold kept a royalty on it. It was a much smaller property when Placer first got involved, and it turned into a million-ounce-a-year mine. That huge royalty basically funded Royal Gold's growth in the acquisition of more properties, and it snowballed from there.

S&A: Do you have any rough guidelines for buying these royalty companies?

Doody: The most important thing to know is that the big ones trade in the market at different multiples than the smaller ones. The big companies tend to trade around 20 times royalties per share.

So if a company has $2 in royalty income per share, the price would tend to average around 20 times that, or $40. Of course, that doesn't mean it can't trade between 15 to 30 times royalty income. Stocks go up and down over the course of the year. But the multiples center around 20.

The smaller companies trade at about half that. In a sense, the public market won't pay the same premium for the small royalty producers that it does for the big ones. And that's probably because there's more risk associated with the smaller ones. They have fewer royalties, so they're more exposed to mine risks. And they don't get to see a lot of big deals, so they tend to get the scraps that the big guys aren't interested in.

Ideally, you want to buy the big ones when they're trading around 15 times royalty income, and sell them when they're trading over 25 times income. And you want to buy the small ones when they're trading around five times royalty income, and sell them when they're trading over 10 times income. But, rather than trading in and out based on the multiple, it can be better to just buy and hold based on their pipeline of growth.

S&A: Any parting thoughts on royalty companies?

Doody: I'll just add that it's common for several of the 10 recommendations in our current "Top 10" portfolio to be royalty companies. That should tell you something about how much we like these stocks.

S&A: Thanks for talking with us, John.

Doody: You're welcome. Thanks for inviting me.

Summary: There are several benefits to owning royalty companies... diversification, relative safety, and high dividends. Those traits allow royalty companies to provide strong, steady growth for investors, with much less risk than the typical mining stock.

HOW TO BUY RARE COINS, ART, AND COLLECTIBLES

This idea is for anyone interested in investing in "real stuff," like gold coins, art, and collectibles.

These hard assets can provide a layer of diversification and inflation protection you can't get from traditional paper investments like stocks, bonds, and exchange-traded funds... But they can also be confusing for new investors.

So we sat down with our favorite expert on "real stuff," Van Simmons, to talk about the things new investors must know before buying. Van is the president of David Hall Rare Coins and is one of the most knowledgeable minds in the world on coins, stamps, and just about any other collectible you can think of.

If you've ever considered investing in these rare items but didn't know where to begin, read on...

Stansberry & Associates: What are the benefits of adding rare coins, art, and collectibles to your investment portfolio?

Van Simmons: Coins, art, and other rare collectibles have several benefits.

First, they're somewhat of an island of safety from currency fluctuations. In other words, their intrinsic value and desirability are not dependent on what's going on with the dollar, the euro, or any other individual currencies.

They're also saleable almost any place on earth in a wide range of currencies, as opposed to many traditional assets that are denominated in dollars or a particular currency.

A second benefit is anonymity. These assets are a way to hold some of your wealth without *Forbes* knowing how wealthy you are.

Things like real estate, stocks, and bonds, can be easily tracked. On the other hand, owning assets like rare coins and art is a way of taking your wealth out of view of almost anyone who wants to know what you own.

Finally, unlike most other investments, these are things that you can actually enjoy. When you invest in a piece of art, you can hang it on your wall and appreciate it every day. You can buy a rare coin, hold it in your hand, and enjoy the history of it. My business partner David Hall has always said that rare coins are literally "history in your hands."

S&A: Are there any keys to successfully investing in these rare assets?

Simmons: There are four big ideas that apply to investing in any of these assets.

First, and probably most important, you need to find a dealer who's honest and is going to treat you fairly.

One thing to look for is a dealer who offers a buy/sell spread and will guarantee to buy a product back. I don't care if it's rare coins, Tiffany lamps, Galle glass, Martin Brothers' pottery, California art, or whatever else... in this business, reputable dealers will agree to buy their products back and tell you exactly what they'll pay for it.

Of course, many dealers will say, "Gee, I'm sorry, we don't buy stuff back." What that usually means is they overcharged you so badly to begin with, they don't want to tell you what they're actually willing to pay you now...

S&A: Do you have any suggestions on how to find a reputable dealer?

Simmons: It really does depend on the market. You can start by talking with and asking questions to a lot of dealers.

You can join clubs in that particular industry and attend events. When you talk to members, inevitably there'll be one or two names that pop up as the most popular dealers.

There are also a million books and websites dedicated to these topics now that can give you a better understanding of your particular market and help you find a dealer you can trust.

If you do your homework – and if you learn what is important and what isn't, or what has value and what doesn't – it makes it hard for a dealer and other collectors to take advantage of you.

In general, it's almost always better to try and work with a dealer who owns a business, as opposed to a salesman. If you deal with the people who own the business, you're dealing with somebody who has a reputation at stake.

There's a reason that I've kept clients for 25 or 30 years... It's because as a business owner, you try to do the best job you can do. If you're dealing with one of the principals of the business, it usually limits your risk. More often than not, they're going to do what's in the client's best interest, because that's in their long-term best interest, also.

S&A: Fair enough. What's the next "big idea"?

Simmons: The second is, you generally want to avoid buying any of these items that are relatively new, whether it's a commemorative plate or a coin that may have just been struck from the Franklin Mint... just about anything that is brand new.

It usually takes 40 or 50 years for something to become a true collectible. So it's a gamble to buy something today hoping in 40 or 50 years it's going to become desirable. There's simply no way to know what's going to be popular 50 years from now.

You're much better off buying something that has a long track record... that has already been a popular collectible for many decades and has a large, well-established collector base. The more popular and the bigger the collector base, generally the more liquid the market is and the better the price will be when you decide you would like to sell.

Of course, these are general guidelines. I've also collected items like old pocket knives where the market is very small – or thinly-traded. But these markets take a little more time and effort to navigate successfully.

Third, you want to buy these items when prices may not have seen much movement for a period of time, or if the market corrects significantly and leaves prices too low.

Like in other markets, these are the times when you're most likely to find items trading at great values. Of course, the hardest thing to do is buy in a bear market. It's not easy to be a contrarian and buy when things are cheap and undervalued... but that's one of the keys to big returns. When you buy a great asset at a great value your chances of success go up exponentially.

Finally – and this is a bit different than some other investments – buy what you like. If you buy an item because it's beautiful, in great condition, and you really like it, chances are, somebody else will like it for similar reasons. So there's an added dimension you don't find in many other assets.

These are the big ideas that investors should focus on, whether they're interested in the most popular items, like rare coins, art, and stamps, or any of the more obscure items, like antique firearms, Navajo rugs, or even pocket knives.

S&A: Let's talk about the big markets in a little more detail. Are there any additional ideas folks should know about investing in rare coins specifically?

Simmons: In the rare coin market – like many other collectibles – another big consideration is condition and grading. You want to buy coins that are graded by a third-party grading service.

I only sell PCGS [Professional Coin Grading Service] coins. Granted, I'm very biased because I helped found the company. But the point is, in most cases, PCGS coins sell for the most money. There's a reason a coin graded by PCGS will sell for $20,000 and a similar coin graded by another company will sell for $10,000 to $15,000 in the same grade.

So you have to buy something that's authentic and correctly evaluated and graded. In the coin market, you don't want to end up with something that's been doctored, tooled, re-toned, or anything else. You want a coin that some third-party authentication group has looked at, verified as being in the correct condition, and will stand behind with a money-back guarantee.

Generally speaking, the better the condition and the rarer the coin, the more the coin will be worth. In most cases, it's best to stay with higher-quality items. If you aren't able to afford a particular high-quality rare coin, it's usually better to consider a different coin than to buy one of lower-quality.

Of course, the very rare items often can't be found in high grades, and ultra-rarities are almost always desirable, regardless of condition. For example, a 1795 $5 Small Eagle – the first U.S. gold coin ever made – has a lot of desirability and value in any grade.

S&A: Are there any other ideas that are particularly important for the art market?

Simmons: In art, you have to deal with a specialist. In paintings especially, you have to make sure what you're buying is authentic, because there are many counterfeits, and really good counterfeits at that. You only want to buy what you know is authentic.

In art, you also want to buy things that have eye appeal. Composition is a huge factor. If a painting is not composed correctly, even people who don't know anything about art can look and see that something's not quite right. So composition makes a big difference... and the era the art is from and the desirability of the artist is also very important.

There's actually a great website you can go to if you'd like to know the value of a particular piece of art. It's called AskArt.com. You can just log on and type in the artist's name and see what all their work has sold for in the last several years. They do require a subscription, but they offer one-day subscriptions if you just have one or two pieces and want to know what they're worth. It's pretty amazing.

S&A: Stamps are another "big" market. Are there any additional considerations with stamps?

Simmons: Like in rare coins, condition is very important in stamps. I was a big buyer of stamps about 10 years ago, and I would only buy stamps that were graded by PSE [Professional Stamp Experts].

In stamps, there are three basic grades: postmarked or canceled, hinged, and never hinged.

Postmarked has been run through a postage meter. Hinged means the stamp has been stuck to an envelope or a stamp book but may still be unused. In the old days, people would often lick a corner of their stamp and stick it in a stamp book. If a particular stamp has never been hinged, it can make five or 10 times the difference in price.

When you're buying stamps, you want to be sure they're well-printed, well-centered, and ideally never hinged. And with some exceptions, most stamps printed after World War I are not particularly rare or collectible.

S&A: Any parting thoughts?

Simmons: Don't try to fool yourself into thinking you know more than the dealer. You aren't going to go out and "steal" something from a dealer. By that I mean it's very difficult to find items that are so mispriced that you can go out and resell the item and make a 20% profit within a day or two.

We travel to coin shows constantly, and we are usually one of the first dealers to hit the trading floor. We'll look at thousands of coins on a given day... and at the end of the day, we may have found one or two coins that are cheaper than usual... where we could resell it to a dealer for a 20% or 30% profit the same day.

Most of the time, our focus is on trying to buy nice, high-quality items trading at fair market prices that can appreciate over the long term. If you do the same, and stick to dealers you trust, it's tough to go wrong.

Really great, high-quality items stay popular for decades and decades. People still collect 1886 Winchesters and Tiffany lamps, and I'm sure they will 100 years from now. Things like that aren't going to change.

S&A: Sounds good. Thanks for talking with us, Van.

Simmons: You're welcome.

Editor's Note: Van is happy to talk with interested S&A readers about making rare coin and collectible investments. You can reach him at 800-759-7575 or 949-567-1325, or via e-mail at info@davidhall.com.

Summary: There are several benefits to adding coins, art, and other rare collectibles to your investment portfolio... First, their value is independent from individual currencies. Second, owning collectible assets takes your wealth out of view of almost anyone who wants to know what you own. And finally, unlike most other investments, these are things that you can actually enjoy. The most important key to successfully investing in these rare assets is to find a dealer who is honest and is going to treat you fairly.

WHY YOU SHOULD HOLD GOLD

This interview is on one of the most popular topics in the newsletter world... gold.

But despite the attention, gold is still grossly misunderstood by most people.

To learn why gold is so valuable – and why it's so important to own – we sat down with Doug Casey, chairman of Casey Research and one of the world's best-known experts on gold and resource investing.

If you still don't own any gold, this interview is required reading. And if you have family or friends who think gold is only for "fringe" types, be sure to pass this along...

Stansberry & Associates: Doug, can you explain why the "idea" of gold is important? Why have we humans used gold as money for thousands of years?

Doug Casey: Well, the truth is, there's nothing magical about gold. It's just uniquely well-suited among the 92 naturally occurring elements for use as money... in the same way aluminum is good for airplanes or uranium is good for nuclear power.

But first we should ask: What is money? It's simply a medium of exchange and a store of value. So lots of different things can and have been used as money for periods of time.

Cows have been used for money. That's where we get the word "pecuniary," from the Latin word for cow, *pecu*. Salt has been used for money, that's where we get the word "salary," from the Latin word for salt, *sal*. Sea shells and cigarettes have been used for money. And of course, paper has often been used for money because it's convenient for governments and political purposes.

But gold is ideally suited because it possesses all five characteristics of good money that Aristotle pointed out back in the fourth-century B.C.

First, it's durable. Money needs to be durable for obvious reasons. It needs to last and not disintegrate in your pocket or in a bank vault. This is why you can't use a commodity like wheat as money... It rots, it can be eaten by pests, and just won't last very long.

Second, gold is divisible. Good money must be divisible to pay for items of different value. It's why you can't use diamonds or famous artwork as money... You can't divide them up without destroying their value.

Third, it's convenient, which is why other elements like copper or lead aren't good money... it takes too much of them to be of value. Can you imagine carrying around hundreds of dollars' worth of copper or lead to make a purchase?

Fourth, gold is consistent. This is why you can't use real estate as money. Every piece of real estate is different from another, whereas one piece of gold is exactly like every other piece of gold.

Finally, and perhaps most importantly, gold has value in and of itself. Paper has next to no intrinsic value of its own, which is why paper is such terrible money.

For all these reasons, I suspect that within a generation – and probably much sooner at this point – gold will again be used as money in day-to-day transactions.

S&A: You mentioned paper money has little intrinsic value. Can you elaborate on why this is so important? Why is paper money in particular so terrible?

Casey: Well, there's actually a sixth reason that Aristotle didn't mention, because it wasn't relevant in his context, but it explains why paper money is so dangerous: a government can't create gold out of nothing.

Not even the worst kings and emperors of Aristotle's time – who routinely clipped and diluted their coins – would have dreamed it possible to pass off worthless paper, which can be created without limit, as money. No one would have accepted paper money for trade.

Yet, that's precisely what the United States started doing when Richard Nixon removed what was left of the dollar gold standard in 1971. Up until then, the U.S. Treasury promised foreigners it would redeem $35 with an ounce of gold, so the dollar was, theoretically, a warehouse receipt for gold. Since 1971, it's literally become an "IOU nothing." And we've been treated to a real-time case study in the dangers of paper money ever since.

Having no real money – gold – in the system allows politicians to come up with all sorts of ridiculous spending programs. There are only three ways a government can get money: taxing – which no one likes; borrowing – which is just putting taxes off to the future, with interest, and inflating the money supply – which drives up prices, but can be blamed on oil companies, farmers, merchants, and anyone else who actually supplies goods and services.

Inflation causes the business cycle, which results in recessions, and eventually depression. It discourages saving, which is how wealth is accumulated. It encourages borrowing, which allows people to live above their means. Inflation makes it easy for governments to finance unpopular wars, like those in Vietnam or Iraq. And inflation will eventually destroy the dollar itself, which will be the ultimate economic catastrophe.

A strictly observed gold standard prevents all these things.

S&A: We've heard why gold is the ideal money. Should it also be viewed as an investment?

Casey: Well, an investment – if we want to define the word – is an allocation of capital to produce more capital. For this reason, gold is not an investment, and has never been an investment.

Gold has been an excellent speculation – which is defined as an allocation of money to profit from politically-caused distortions in the economic system – from time to time over the past four decades. But it's never been an investment.

Gold shares can be an investment because you're allocating capital in a mine to produce more wealth in the form of gold. But gold itself is not.

I consider gold to be cash in its most basic form, much more so than the U.S. paper currency we currently call money.

So in the same way it's always good to keep some savings in U.S. dollars – or whichever paper currency you're currently obligated to use – it's always good to keep some savings in gold.

S&A: That's great advice. Thanks for talking with us, Doug.

Casey: You're welcome. It was my pleasure.

Summary: Gold is money... because it is durable, divisible, convenient, consistent, valuable, and cannot be created out of thin air by the government. Just as it's always a good idea to keep some savings in your local currency, it's also a good idea to keep some savings in gold.

MASTERING THE RESOURCE MARKET'S CYCLICALITY

If you plan to invest one dime in natural resources like gold, oil, and uranium, this interview is a must read.

We sat down with legendary resource investor Rick Rule to discuss how one can master the giant cycles in natural resources. Catch one of these big cycles early, and you may never have to work again. Catch one at the wrong time, and you'll lose a fortune...

Rick has spent decades in the resource markets, making himself and his clients many millions of dollars in the process. He has also financed several of the most important resource companies in the world. He's a brilliant trader, a genius investor, and a walking encyclopedia of business knowledge.

If you're looking to make life-changing profits from commodities or resource stocks, read on...

Stansberry & Associates: Rick, most readers are aware of how profitable investing in commodities and natural resource stocks can be. The gains on individual positions can run into the thousands, even tens of thousands of percent. But many people are unaware of the cyclical nature of resources... and how to use this aspect to efficiently invest or speculate in them. Could you explain how a resource cycle works?

Rick Rule: Sure. Resource markets are cyclical for two primary reasons... They are extremely capital intensive, and they are extremely time intensive. In other words, resources tend to take a great deal of time and money to produce, mine, or extract.

So when supply and demand imbalances occur, the resource sector isn't able to react as quickly as other markets. This long lag time creates huge price swings... extreme highs and extreme lows you don't see in most other markets.

When demand exceeds supply in most markets, you see a relatively quick reaction from producers to meet the new demand. Compare this to resources like copper or gold... Before you can produce it, you have to go find it and build a mine. The exploration cycle – the pre-development cycle – can take up to 10 years. In the meantime, prices can soar while the market waits for that increased supply.

On the other side, after supplies come onto the market, prices peak and start to fall. What happens is that the industry comes to regard their sunk costs as just that... sunk costs. So they're hesitant to slow production, in spite of high supplies and falling prices. They'll continue to produce even when prices fall below the level at which they would be profitable. In fact, they'll often produce even below the marginal cost of production for a while in a contest known in the resource industry as "the last man standing."

The reasoning here is that it might cost them more to shut down a project and restart it than it would to continue operating at a loss. And each producer wants to be the first in the game when the cycle turns back around. This drives prices even lower than they otherwise would go.

So you have this extraordinary cyclicality as a consequence of the capital and time intensive nature of the business.

S&A: Can you give us a couple examples of resource cycles in action?

Rule: Sure... To give your readers a feel for the extremes of commodity cycles, let's look at uranium.

In the 1970s, uranium prices kept pace with other energy sources, escalating tenfold. And uranium share prices exceeded those commodity price escalations.

But the decline in energy prices that accompanied the worldwide economic slowdown in the early 1980s – along with the "Three Mile Island" mishap – delivered a staggering blow to uranium markets.

Then the Chernobyl disaster finished them off.

The uranium bear market – beginning in 1992 and ending in 2002 – saw the uranium price decline from $35 per pound to $7 per pound. At the bottom of the market, the industry was selling the stuff for $7-$9 per pound and producing it for $18 per pound. They were losing $10 per pound and trying to make it up on volume!

Worldwide however, we were producing 90 million pounds and consuming 150 million pounds, with the consumed surplus coming from prior excess utility inventories, and conversion of weapons-grade stocks. So the price had to rebound, and it did.

In the period from 2002-2006, the spot price soared from $7 to $130. Meanwhile, production costs approximately doubled to $40 per pound. Since then, the price of uranium has continued to fluctuate dramatically.

The reaction of investors to these cycles is amusing, if tragic.

At the periodic highs, investors were crowding frantically into uranium equities, although the stage was set – through price induced increases in supply and reductions in demand – for a price collapse. And of course, investors sold in disgust at market lows, when inverse conditions argued for dramatic increases in the uranium price.

S&A: Are there any tricks for distinguishing where we are in a particular commodity's cycle?

Rule: Yes... In any resource, when the industry's median production cost exceeds the commodity's selling price – in other words when it costs companies more to produce that commodity than the commodity is worth on the market – that industry is in liquidation. This is the situation I just mentioned in uranium.

There are two potential outcomes at that point... either the price has to rise, or that commodity will no longer be for sale on the market. That is a strong sign that you're approaching or have arrived at the bottom of a cycle.

Conversely, when commodity producers as a whole enjoy 50% or better pre-tax margins and returns on capital employed exceed the S&P 500's returns on employed capital by 50% or more, you should be looking for the exits. The stage is set for a serious decline in the price on that commodity.

In other words, markets work. The cure for low prices is low prices, and the cure for high prices is high prices.

S&A: You've made a career of profiting from resource cyclicality. What advice do you have for readers to do the same?

Rule: Well, technically it's as simple as following the old Wall Street adage of "buy low and sell high." You want to buy when supply exceeds demand and prices are low, and sell when demand exceeds supply and prices are high. It sounds easy. But in practice, it's very difficult to follow.

Most people don't have the courage to buy something that is dirt-cheap and has gone nowhere for years... But that's what it takes to "buy low" in the resource sector. Similarly, most people don't have the discipline to sell something that has soared hundreds or thousands of percent... But that's what it takes to "sell high."

So the first thing that one must do is learn to master him or herself before attempting to master cyclicality.

Warren Buffett famously said you shouldn't buy a share of stock unless you know it well enough that you would be delighted to see it fall 25% in price, so you could buy more at a 25% discount.

That is also how you must approach the resource sector. Even when you buy low, it is certain many of your investments will go lower before they go higher. You absolutely will buy shares of XYZ exploration for $1 a share and see it fall to $0.70 a share. If you did your research, the stock will be a substantially better buy at $0.70 a share than it was at $1 a share, and you need to buy it.

When you buy resource stocks, you need to recognize that they're not merely trading vehicles. They represent fractional ownership of a business.

And to profit from them, I think you have to go through the type of analysis your colleague Dan Ferris goes through.

What's the company worth? If the company is worth $1 billion and there are 10 million shares outstanding, what is the value per share of the business?

That's a simple example, but many people don't go even that far.

If you have a good sense of what something is worth, and it declines in price... you may have the courage and the sense to buy more. If it escalates fairly rapidly in price to the point where its price exceeds your estimate of its value, you might make a rational sell decision.

But without that sort of grounding in value and understanding, most people have no business in resource stocks.

S&A: Thanks for the insight, Rick.

Rule: You're welcome. Thanks for having me.

Summary: To profit from resource cyclicality, you want to buy when supply exceeds demand and prices are low, and sell when demand exceeds supply and prices are high. Since resource stocks represent fractional ownership of a business, you must determine what the company is worth before buying the shares.

TIMBERLAND

Most people have never considered the idea of investing in timberland... and that's a mistake.

In this interview, Dr. Steve Sjuggerud reveals why timberland is one of his all-time favorite "alternative" investments.

If you're like most investors, you're looking for ways to earn big, safe long-term returns. This interview will show you a great way to do so... while diversifying your money outside of the U.S. dollar and traditional investments.

Stansberry & Associates: You've done a tremendous amount of research on timberland investing over the years... and you've been a big proponent of this idea. You've called it "the ultimate agriculture investment." What is so special about timberland?

Steve Sjuggerud: Yes... I've literally been all over the world researching timberland investing. I've spent hundreds of hours on it. I've recommended many timber stocks to my readers over the years. And I've personally invested in timberland.

There's a long list of reasons why investing in timberland is a great idea... and consistently produces big returns.

First of all, trees grow year in and year out. Trees in good growing regions in the U.S. grow at 6%-8% per year. They grow through recessions. They grow through wars. They grow through stock and real estate crashes. They grow through everything. They give you built-in investment growth that isn't guaranteed with a stock.

Along with the tree growth, the price of wood has grown at a consistent rate throughout the years. It's extremely difficult for a company to increase the prices of its goods by 6% every year, but the price of wood, according to legendary money manager Jeremy Grantham, has increased by that amount for the last 100 years. Specifically, he says "stumpage" prices – the value of all the wood on the stump – have beaten inflation by 3% a year over the last century.

Another nice thing is timberland is a resource investment, but it's not a constantly depleting one, like a gold mine or an oil well. Trees will grow back. It's a sustainable resource investment.

And not to ramble on, but you should know, timber is uncorrelated to the stock market. It makes sense... the trees have never heard of the Nasdaq bubble... and they don't know what a "War on Terror" is. This makes timber a great place to park money in big portfolios... where you need diversification.

S&A: But what happens to your timberland investment in a down year, when lumber prices crash?

Sjuggerud: That's a great question. What happens when the market is slumping? When you can't get the price you need to make the business profitable? Did you just waste eight... 15... 25 years on an investment with nothing to show for it? The answer can be summed up in five words: "*Bank it on the stump.*"

In the industry, it's a phrase that means if conditions aren't right for harvesting your crop, you just keep letting it grow. You keep the profits on the stump and wait for a more profitable time to sell your timber – most likely, when timber prices are in your favor.

One of the great benefits of owning timberland is you don't have to harvest it every year. It's not like fruit, where it's ripe just once and then you have to pick it. Instead, it grows exponentially on the stump for years.

This is not to imply that timber is an absolutely risk-free investment... But with the ability to bank it on the stump, investing in timber does come with an extra safety net. "If the rain rains, the sun shines, the suckers grow," Jeremy Grantham once said. "If you don't want to sell, they get bigger and more expensive."

S&A: Those are tremendous attributes. How has timberland performed over the years?

Sjuggerud: Take a look at this table of the period from 1971 to 2010... which was filled with all sorts of bull and bear markets for stocks...

Year Annual	Return Account	Size
1971	4.4%	$10,000
1972	11.0%	$11,104
1973	58.7%	$17,625
1974	20.8%	$21,290
1975	1.3%	$21,564
1976	16.0%	$25,021
1977	48.5%	$37,154
1978	29.5%	$48,103
1979	31.0%	$62,991
1980	5.4%	$66,405
1981	1.6%	$68,132
1982	-1.8%	$66,919
1983	0.6%	$67,294
1984	3.2%	$69,434
1985	-2.6%	$67,656
1986	3.3%	$69,916
1987	26.6%	$88,513
1988	30.1%	$115,174
1989	37.4%	$158,191
1990	11.1%	$175,687
1991	20.3%	$211,281
1992	37.3%	$290,131
1993	22.4%	$355,033
1994	15.4%	$409,850
1995	13.8%	$466,574
1996	10.7%	$516,637
1997	18.9%	$614,333
1998	9.0%	$669,746
1999	12.9%	$756,344
2000	4.4%	$789,681

Year Annual	Return Account	Size
2001	-5.2%	$748,256
2002	1.9%	$762,340
2003	7.7%	$820,773
2004	11.2%	$912,697
2005	19.3%	$1,089,288
2006	13.7%	$1,238,287
2007	18.4%	$1,466,549
2008	9.5%	$1,606,184
2009	-4.8%	$1,529,730
2010	-0.2%	$1,527,309

From 1971-2010, an investor in timber saw average annual returns of over 14% – turning $10,000 into over $1.5 million. That's better than stocks and bonds over the same period.

Here are the rough numbers on where timberland returns come from:

- 1% Land value increase
- 6% Biologic growth of the trees
- 3% "Stumpage" price increase (the price of the actual tree)

S&A: So timberland can serve as a good alternative investment when stocks are in a bear market?

Sjuggerud: Absolutely. One of the worst-ever bear markets in stocks began in the late 1960s and lasted until about 1980. An investor in stocks during that time lost money, due to inflation.

However, as the table shows, an investor in timber never had a losing year during that period. More often than not, the returns were in the double-digits... with a 59% return in 1973 and a 49% return in 1977.

To sum up, timberland offers high returns... It is a sustainable asset that can provide returns for centuries... It has no correlation to the stock market... It's less volatile... And it constantly grows in value.

S&A: So, how do you go about buying timberland? What's the easiest way to own it?

Sjuggerud: It's important to point out that rather than just going out and buying a forest, you want to make sure to invest in *managed timberland.*

The reason it's important to make the distinction is simple: Managed timberlands, according to a study conducted by the University of Georgia and published in the *Journal of Forestry*, generate returns almost four times higher than non-managed lands.

With managed timberlands, you get just what it says. You get professional managers who cultivate the trees, look after them, and harvest the trees and their products at the right time.

They look to earn extra cash by selling hunting rights to the land. They harvest and sell the straw and seeds that fall from the trees. Good managers even look to sell chunks of your timberland if a real estate developer comes along and offers a sky-high premium for your land.

My point is everything on the "tree farm" – even the tree farm itself – is for sale. You can make these types of managed timberland investments privately, or there are usually a handful of publicly traded timberland companies on the exchange at any given time.

The big names in the U.S. are Weyerhaeuser (WY), Rayonier (RYN), and Plum Creek (PCL). To spread your risk, you can buy the U.S. big names through an exchange-traded fund with the symbol: WOOD. You can get much broader international exposure through the Guggenheim timber ETF (symbol: CUT).

S&A: There are many good points to timberland investing. Any negative ones?

Sjuggerud: When you compare the built-in yield of timberland to any other asset class out there, timberland wins hands-down.

The only problem is *time frame* – you can sell a stock or bond immediately, but you can't get rid of acres of timber like that. It's illiquid. You've got to hold it for some time to maximize its value – the ideal timeframe is infinity. It's definitely not for traders... it's for long-term thinking investors.

And keep in mind... like all investments, you have to make sure you buy timberland at a reasonable price.

S&A: Thanks, Steve.

Sjuggerud: You're welcome.

Summary: Why invest in timberland? First, trees grow year in and year out. The price of wood also has grown at a consistent rate throughout the years. Next, timberland is a sustainable resource investment. It's not a constantly depleting one like a gold mine or an oil well. Finally, timber is uncorrelated to the stock market. This makes timber a great place to diversify big portfolios.

BUYING DISCOUNTED CORPORATE BONDS

This interview is with Porter Stansberry, founder of Stansberry & Associates Investment Research.

We sat down with Porter to discuss one of his favorite investment strategies. It's an idea he says literally changed his investing life, and one he thinks all investors should become familiar with – buying discounted corporate bonds.

We know most investors think buying bonds is about as exciting as watching paint dry, but this idea may surprise you. Porter says when the conditions are right, you can double your money while taking on zero risk.

To learn how, read on...

Stansberry & Associates: Porter, you've written a great deal about corporate bonds. In fact, you've gone so far as to say that learning the correct way to buy them will literally change an investor's life. What's so great about buying discounted corporate bonds?

Porter Stansberry: Well, it's probably better to begin by describing what's *not* so great about buying stocks.

Stocks are really only worth what you can sell them for in the market, or what they'll pay you in dividends over time. But there are two problems with this... Neither of those values is guaranteed.

First, there is no guarantee that when you go to the market other people will pay what you expect for your stock. In fact, there's no guarantee they'll pay *anything* for your stock.

Secondly, there is no guarantee that you're going to receive the dividends you expect. Dividend policy is totally the domain of the board of directors. Unfortunately, in public companies, most boards are terrible... Most simply don't care about shareholders. So, you're truly at the mercy of the board... or at the mercy of the marketplace.

Frankly, that doesn't sit well with me... which is why I only buy stocks when they're extremely cheap or have proven track records of paying dividends. Unfortunately, that means many times there's just nothing for me to buy.

S&A: So what are the advantages of buying bonds?

Stansberry: The advantages of buying bonds are precisely that you do get those guarantees... You're guaranteed to get some percentage of your invested capital back. You're guaranteed to receive a dividend.

In simple terms, a bond is nothing more than a loan... It's a loan that you make to a corporation in the form of a security. Say you buy a typical $1,000 bond. That means the company agrees to pay you back your $1,000 in full at a certain point in the future. It can be a short-term loan or a longer-term loan... It could be 30 days or seven years. There are all kinds of different terms and periods. But the most important thing is that at the end of the term, the company – by law – is required to pay par, which means the full price of the bond as it was underwritten.

Believe it or not, sometimes you can go out in the marketplace and find bonds that by law are obligated to repay investors $1,000, but that are trading for $800, $700, sometimes even $500 or $400. These are referred to as discounted corporate bonds.

By the way, some new investors are confused by the lingo here. In the bond market, they don't say these bonds are trading at $800... They say they're trading at $80. They don't say they're trading at $500... They say they're trading at $50. A simple way to think about this is to multiply the terms by 10 to get the real dollar amount... For example, $80 multiplied by 10 is $800.

The amazing thing about these discounted bonds is you have a legal claim on that corporation to be repaid in full... a *legal* claim. It's not a matter of what the market will decide to pay you. The company has to pay you back in full, or else it goes bankrupt and all the assets the company has are sold off and the value of that sale is distributed to all the bondholders.

Now, I'm not suggesting you want to buy bonds that are going to go bankrupt. That usually ends up being a painfully long process, and it might take you years to get your money back. That's not the idea.

The idea is to find bonds where the assets can clearly cover the bondholders so that bankruptcy does not have to occur. Instead, asset sales will happen and the company will pay back the bond-holders without going bankrupt. You see this happen all the time.

So when you choose the right bonds, you're basically guaranteed to get a good return on your investment.

S&A: And the second advantage?

Stansberry: The second advantage of bonds is they pay a fixed coupon. Remember, I said the other problem with stocks is their dividends are decided by the board of directors. The truth is that most stocks don't pay any dividends at all, and often times if they do, they're so small it's hardly worth it.

But you can know exactly what a bond will pay you because the interest payment – it's called a coupon for bonds, rather than a dividend as it is for stocks – is fixed. You know exactly when and exactly how much you're going to get paid... so you can know exactly what the yield will be from your investment.

S&A: Can you give us an example of how this works?

Stansberry: Sure... Let's say you buy a particular corporate bond at a discount. You pay $0.80 on the dollar, and the term of the bond is one year. You know that one year from now you're going to make a profit of $0.20 on the dollar, because you're buying it at $0.80, and you're going to get a full $1 when the company pays you, because the bond has to be paid back at par. If par is $1,000, then you're paying $800 for the bond.

So, right off the bat you know you're going to make $200, or 25% on your money that year. That's a pretty good return, and it's guaranteed by the company... it's a legal obligation. But it gets even better.

The second way you're going to get paid is over the course of the year you're going to get coupon payments. On a fully priced bond, a coupon might be 8%... so in this case you're going to get a total of $80 from the bond that year. That's another $80 on your original $800 investment, or an additional 10% return on your original capital invested. In total, on this one deal, you're going to make 35% on your money.

What is the risk that you took on this deal? The risk in this case was the company would go bankrupt and would have to repay you over time. Instead of getting your money back in a year, it might take two or three years. That's no good... We don't want that. But it's a heck of a lot better than if you buy a stock and it goes bankrupt and you get nothing back ever.

Again, the idea is not to buy bonds that will go bankrupt, but to buy bonds where the company has plenty of assets available to repay their bondholders without having to go bankrupt. That's the essence of buying corporate bonds at a discount.

S&A: Are there any important strategies for buying these bonds that we need to know about?

Stansberry: Well, there's a wrinkle to the process that I want to discuss, because it's the real secret behind the people who make a lot of money in bonds.

The average recovery rate for corporate bonds that have gone bankrupt over the last 50 years or so is about $0.45 on the dollar.

So, if your bond goes bankrupt, chances are you'll get about $0.45 on the dollar... Sometimes you might get less, sometimes you might get more.

This is where being an analyst becomes important. You have to know what the liquidation value of the corporation is. An analyst spends all his time figuring this out: What is this company worth if the worst happens and it goes bankrupt? Can we get our money back? That's the big consideration before you buy any discounted bond.

But forget all that for now... Let's assume you don't know any of those things. You decide you're going to buy a bond at $60. Since we know the average recovery rate is $0.45 on the dollar, if the bond does go bankrupt, your expected loss is about $15. So you are taking a 25% risk, but what are you getting in return?

In return you're getting the right to be paid the par for that bond if it doesn't go bankrupt... You'll make $40 on a $60 investment. Now, again, these are bond market terms... The reality is the bond costs $1,000, you're going to invest $600, and you're going to get a $400 profit for doing so. That's more than a 65% return... a huge gain.

You're risking $150 to get $400... That's a much better risk-to-return ratio than you'll find in the stock market. You're always risking less in bonds... and if you buy discounted bonds you can actually make profits that are larger than average in the stock market. This is why many of the richest people in the world spend more time and money on bonds than they do on stocks.

S&A: If the risks are so low with these bonds, why do they often trade at such big discounts?

Stansberry: One of the big reasons corporate bonds trade at such a big discount is because a lot of institutions that own bonds – like insurance companies, pension funds, and a lot of bond funds, banks, and brokers – are not allowed to own them if the bonds lose their investment-grade credit rating.

When a company stumbles or has a couple bad quarters, the bonds can get marked down by Moody's and Standard & Poor's. They can go from investment-grade rated to what's called junk-rated. But junk-rated doesn't mean what most people think. It doesn't mean that the company is "junk," it simply means that the company's cash earnings necessary to fully cover the bond's coupons are becoming jeopardized.

It doesn't mean that the coupons won't get paid. It doesn't mean that the company will go into bankruptcy. It means nothing at all about the future recovery value of those bonds. All it means is that this company has stumbled, its earnings are weaker, and there is a greater chance – far from guaranteed – that they'll miss a coupon payment.

So when that happens – when there's any chance of a missed payment at all – the company goes from investment-grade to non-investment grade, and all these institutions are forced to sell... There's an entire cohort of the largest money pools in the world that can no longer own them, and they tumble in price.

This is where people like myself and a lot of other smart investors – the so-called "vulture investors" – can pick up fantastic opportunities.

The professional investors who specialize in discounted corporate bonds tend to be the smartest people on Wall Street and tend to be the most rigorous about what they pay. Not coincidentally, they also tend to make the most money.

S&A: Is there anything else we should know about discounted corporate bonds?

Stansberry: There is one last thing that I want readers to understand.

If you're buying a stock that was trading at $100 six months ago and now it's trading at $5, the odds are that stock is going to zero.

Stocks that go from $100 to below $5 rarely get back above $5. Those kinds of losses usually only happen if there's a serious problem in that company. Serious problems are bad news for stockholders, because they have no real claims in bankruptcy. So sometimes when you think you're buying a super-cheap stock, you're actually taking a huge risk... where there's an excellent chance that you'll end up with nothing.

This is the fun part about bonds... The lower the price of a bond, the more likely you'll make money. It sounds unbelievable, but it's true. The lower the price of the bond, the lower the risk, because the closer it gets to the recovery price.

For example, I personally made a lot of money buying bonds in

General Motors. This is somewhat ironic because I had been predicting for years that General Motors would go bankrupt... and of course it did.

But after it went bankrupt, I was able to buy its bonds for between $0.15 and $0.20 on the dollar. I had done my homework, and I knew the liquidation value of the bonds would be somewhere around $0.40 on the dollar.

Well, along came the Obama administration... They completely ignored all the bankruptcy laws, and they ended up giving 40% of the company to the unions, which was unbelievable and unheard of.

Because of that, the bonds only ended up being worth about $0.30 on the dollar at bankruptcy, rather than the $0.40 on the dollar they otherwise would have been. I ended up making less than expected, but I still almost doubled my money in 18 months with no risk.

Now, I'm sure some people will think, "What do you mean you had no risk? You're buying bonds in bankruptcy, of course you had risk." But the fact is I didn't.

I knew what the bonds would be worth in bankruptcy, and I knew the bankruptcy process would not last a decade. So, I had no real risk. If more people understood this, it would completely change their financial futures.

S&A: Thanks for talking with us.

Stansberry: My pleasure.

Summary: Discounted corporate bonds are the closest thing to a "perfect" investment you'll find in the market. They offer a better risk-to-reward ratio than stocks, commodities, or any other common investment. Buying corporate bonds at a discount to their liquidation value is the only guaranteed way to earn substantial returns without putting your capital at risk.

BUYING CLOSED-END FUNDS AT A DISCOUNT

As the editor behind the hugely successful *Retirement Millionaire* advisory, Dr. David Eifrig has studied every kind of investment.

One of his favorite "no risk" ways to make money... a strategy he calls "the closest thing to free money," is buying closed-end funds. It's one of the most useful and most misunderstood investment vehicles in the world. As you'll see, closed-end funds are well worth adding to your investment "toolbox."

Stansberry & Associates: Doc, you've called the strategy of buying closed-end funds one of the few legitimate "free money opportunities" in the investment markets. Before we talk about how this idea works, can you first define what a closed-end fund is?

Dr. David Eifrig: Sure. Basically, there are two types of funds available to general investors: open-end funds and closed-end funds. Most of the funds folks are familiar with, like the traditional mutual funds you might own in a 401(k), are open-end funds.

"Open-end" means the fund will issue as many shares as investors are willing to buy. When investors put more money into the fund, the fund issues more shares and buys more shares of the underlying stocks. Because of this, the price you pay for a share of an open-end fund will always be the total value of the stocks in the fund divided by the current number of shares outstanding. This value is known as the "net asset value," or NAV. Open-end funds always trade at their NAV.

Closed-end funds work differently. These funds issue a limited number of shares. If you want to buy these shares, you must go into the stock market where they trade like a normal stock. In other words, to buy a closed-end fund, by definition someone else must sell their shares.

As a result, the value of a closed-end fund can fluctuate significantly and the share price does not necessarily reflect the NAV. Any difference between the share price and NAV of a closed-end fund is known as the premium or discount, depending on if the share price is higher or lower than the NAV.

In theory, this situation makes no sense. Closed-end funds should never trade at a discount, and they certainly shouldn't trade at a premium. After all, it would be foolish to sell a fund for less than it's actually worth... And it definitely makes no sense to buy a fund for more than it's worth.

Of course... in the real world, it does happen. Whether it's because someone has to sell for reasons unrelated to the fund, such as a margin call, or folks irrationally selling out of fear, like we saw in 2008 and 2009... closed-end funds will sometimes sell at a significant discount to NAV. This can be a huge opportunity for investors.

S&A: Why is buying these funds at a discount such a great idea?

Eifrig: It's because under most circumstances, the fund's share price will return to NAV. One of two things is going to happen... Either the market will realize the fund is underpriced and drive the share price up, or the fund managers will get shareholder approval to buy back shares and remove the discount.

Either way, the share price is almost certain to rise. All you have to do is buy it, hold it, and wait.

S&A: How can investors take advantage of these fluctuations in closed-end funds?

Eifrig: The first step is discovering these situations when they exist. There are a couple great ways to do this.

Barron's publishes a list of closed-end fund valuations. I follow this weekly and you can as well – it can be found in the "M" or market section. It tracks the amount of money going in and out of the funds, the net asset values, and the discounts or premiums to NAVs.

There's also a great free website you can use. It's www.CEFconnect.com, where the CEF stands for closed-end fund. You can go there and find almost any screen you can imagine. You can sort by fund type, market cap, discount or premium to NAV, and a number of other variables. It's a fantastic resource.

S&A: Do you have any guidelines on when to buy these funds?

Eifrig: There are no hard and fast rules, but there are a few important points.

First, you need to consider the type of fund. If we're talking about funds that hold bonds or large-cap stocks, I'll get interested when they're trading at 7% or 8% discounts, because those assets are well-traded and highly liquid. On the other hand, if the fund invests in emerging-market stocks or other illiquid or opaquely priced assets, I need to see 12%-15% discounts before I even consider buying.

Occasionally, if you're patient, you'll find incredible situations where funds holding safe, liquid assets are trading at discounts of 10%, 15%, or even more.

A great example here was municipal bonds in 2009. At the time, everyone was talking about the collapse of the municipal-bond market, so investors who held those bonds started selling them en masse, including closed-end funds. So we saw a number of them trading at 15% or 16% discounts.

But when we looked at the facts, we could see the fears were overblown, and the market was offering a huge opportunity. Buying those bonds at a 15% discount was like buying a tax-free dollar for $0.85. And all we had to do was sit and wait for them to return to NAV to make a safe and easy double-digit gain.

Most of these funds hold assets like stocks, bonds, and other funds which are easy to price, so it's relatively easy to determine the NAV. The key is to figure whether there is a legitimate reason for the discount – which is rare – or if the market is simply mispricing the fund. If it's the latter, these are some of the best, safest opportunities available to individual investors.

S&A: When should you sell these funds?

Eifrig: Again, there are no set rules for selling, but whenever I see a fund go from a significant discount to any type of premium, I'll start looking to sell.

One thing to consider is whether all the funds in that sector are now trading at a premium or if it's just that particular fund. If it's just the one, I may consider selling it and buying another fund in the same sector that's still trading at a discount. You might be surprised how often that happens.

S&A: Are there any significant risks to buying discounted closed-end funds?

Eifrig: There are no additional risks to buying these funds, but naturally, they're subject to the same risks as any other investment.

If the stocks, bonds, or other assets in a fund fall in value, the value of the fund could fall, too. Buying these funds at a significant discount provides a degree of additional safety, but it's always possible that funds trading at a discount could go on to trade at an even bigger discount.

There is one additional factor you should consider, though, and that is leverage. Because the market is offering such low yields right now, some funds are using leverage to increase their yields. For example, a fund may invest in bonds yielding 3%, and lever 50% of the funds to increase the yield to 4.5%. Leverage in and of itself is not a problem, but you should avoid funds with excessive leverage. I recommend staying under 30% leverage in any fund.

What's great is you can use the CEFconnect website I mentioned earlier to see exactly how much leverage any fund uses, so it's easy to find the funds you want.

S&A: Sounds great. Any parting thoughts?

Eifrig: It's funny... I actually remember the first time I heard about closed-end funds. I remember exactly where I was. I was driving in an old '63 Electra, and I was listening to some radio talk show. They started talking about closed-end funds and discounts to NAV, and I literally had to pull over on the side of the road. I had never heard anything like it.

I thought it was such a profound, easy way to make money. Here was a way to buy an asset that's worth $1 for just $0.80 or $0.90, and all you had to do was hold it and wait.

After all these years, it's still one of my favorite strategies. Buying closed-end funds at a discount is one of the few legitimate ways to make nearly risk-free money in the investment markets... It's the closest thing to free money you'll find.

S&A: Thanks for talking with us, Doc.

Eifrig: You're welcome.

Summary: Buying closed-end funds at a discount to their "net asset value" is a great idea because under most circumstances, the fund's share price will return to NAV... Either the market will realize the fund is underpriced and drive the share price up, or the fund managers will get shareholder approval to buy back shares and remove the discount. Either way, the share price is almost certain to rise. All you have to do is buy it, hold it, and wait.

SUMMARY AND RECOMMENDED READING

If you've made it this far, you're now familiar with the world's most powerful investment ideas.

But keep in mind, this book's goal is to provide an "introduction" to each idea... not to delve deeply into it.

If you're interested in learning more about wealth, investment, trading, and economics, there are many fantastic books out there.

Collectively, Stansberry & Associates' analysts have read over 1,000 books about these ideas.

Below, you'll find our favorites. We've categorized them into "Investing," "Wealth Building & Personal Success," "Trading," and "History & Economics."

We believe these books will help make you a much better investor.

Investing

Beating the Street

A great book from Peter Lynch. It goes into detail about specific industries. Lynch also offers his 25 golden rules of investing, which are incredibly valuable.

Bull: A History of the Boom and Bust

A well-written book about the 2000 stock market crash... and the people who saw it coming.

Crisis Investing for the Rest of the '90s

Timeless lessons in money, markets, and philosophy from expert investor Doug Casey.

Devil Take the Hindmost: A History of Financial Speculation

The best book on financial bubbles... a much easier read than Extraordinary Popular Delusions and the Madness of Crowds.

The Essays of Warren Buffett: Lessons for Corporate America

Warren Buffett is one of the greatest investors of all time. His writings on business, investment, and wealth are priceless. You'll find them in this collection.

F Wall Street

An easy-to-read guide for how to identify and value great businesses.

Fooled by Randomness

With stories about the huge role randomness plays in life, Nassim Nicholas Taleb takes the wind out of Wall Street's sails.

Hedgehogging

A great collection of stories by famed hedge-fund manager/analyst Barton Biggs.

Hot Commodities

Jim Rogers, the master, on the basics of commodity investing... and his favorite ways to play the commodity boom.

The Intelligent Investor

Frequently cited as one of the ultimate books on investing. The most important pieces of advice are in Chapter 20 (about margin of safety) and Chapter 8 (the story of Mr. Market).

Investment Biker

The legendary Jim Rogers' first book. International finance, wild travel stories, and investment 101 in South America, Europe, Asia, Australia, and Africa. All on motorcycles.

Liar's Poker

Michael Lewis' classic story of rising through the Solomon Brothers' system.

The Little Book that Still Beats the Market

Easy to read and easy to understand; it'll teach you a simple investment approach that boils down to: buy good businesses, but only at cheap prices.

Margin of Safety

Seth Klarman is one of the greatest stock-market investors of all time. Margin of Safety describes his contrarian approach.

The Mind of Wall Street

The late Leon Levy made a fortune on Wall Street. This book is full of real stories explaining how he did it.

The Most Important Thing: Uncommon Sense for the Thoughtful Investor

Written by one of the great investors of our time, Howard Marks, this is an easy-to-read book full of timeless common sense.

One Up on Wall Street

This book will teach you how to think about the overall stock market and how to spot good businesses to buy. Peter Lynch is famous for encouraging investors to buy what they understand.

Practical Speculation

Victor Niederhoffer's chapter on technical analysis alone is worth the price of the book.

Street Smarts

Legendary investor Jim Rogers on the latest form of currency control, the most exciting economies in the world, and what assets you can buy to profit from government money printing.

Wall Street Meat

Andy Kessler's first-hand account of the late-'90s tech boom.

Winning on Wall Street

Martin Zweig is one of the greatest market analysts ever. Learn how he does it.

What Works on Wall Street

Author James O'Shaughnessy crunched a lot of data to produce this book... which reveals the few stock market approaches that actually work.

You Can Be a Stock Market Genius

This book details specific, useful approaches to stock investing that most people never use. It's considered required reading in the hedge-fund industry.

Wealth Building & Personal Success

How to Win Friends and Influence People

This is a classic, must-read book on how to be successful. It will be relevant 100 years from now.

The Richest Man in Babylon

One of the top 10 all-time classics on wealth-building and success.

How to Get Rich

A modern classic on building wealth. Felix Dennis is a unique author: an entertaining, expert wealth-builder who is also a great writer.

How to Be Rich

This is no "get rich quick" book. It's a book about the attitudes, beliefs, and habits that produce wealth. This classic was written over 40 years ago, but it will be relevant forever.

Trading

Market Wizards

Interviews with the best traders and investors in the world. The Jim Rogers interview might be the most important 40 pages you'll ever read about investing.

The New Market Wizards

More interviews with the best traders and investors in the world.

Reminiscences of a Stock Operator

At his height in the 1920s, Jesse Livermore was one of the most successful traders in the world. This account of Livermore making and losing huge fortunes contains the commandments of speculation.

Trade Your Way to Financial Freedom

The two major lessons to learn from this book: How to exit a trade, and how much money to place in one.

Pit Bull

Few people can make a dime by independently trading short-term market movements. Martin Schwartz made millions doing it. Pit Bull is his book. The story about his wife's mink coat is hilarious.

Trader Vic: Methods of a Wall Street Master

Vic Sperandeo is an encyclopedia of market information and history. He used his knowledge to string together a 10-year stretch of annualized 70% gains that started in the late '70s. Learn his methods here.

The Options Workbook

This is a solid resource for learning options basics. You'll learn options in no time if you make use of the "workbook" aspect.

History & Economics

A History of The American People

Paul Johnson is one of S&A's favorite historians. This is his excellent, comprehensive book on U.S. history.

The Big Short

This is Michael Lewis' book on the people who made a fortune during the 2008 credit crisis. It's one of the most entertaining financial books ever written.

Gold: The Once and Future Money

A great book on the history of gold and its use as currency.

Eat the Rich

Force your children to read this book and learn how the world really works. It's the best explanation of economics available... and it's hilarious.

Economics in One Lesson

This classic book is a rarity. It's an easy-to-read, common sense guide to economics.

Empire of Debt

A great piece of financial history. This book describes how the U.S. is borrowing and spending its way to the poorhouse.

Modern Times

Another great history book from Paul Johnson. This one covers the world from the 1920s through the 1990s. It tells story after story of how big government doesn't work.

The Power of Gold

A great history of gold and mankind's lust for it.

World War I: The Rest of the Story and How It Affects You Today

Author Richard Maybury is a national treasure. We encourage you and your children to read his books over and over. They are a pleasure to read. This one covers World War I.

World War II: The Rest of the Story and How It Affects You Today

This Richard Maybury book covers World War II.

The State of Africa: A History of the Continent Since Independence

This history of post-World War II Africa is full of interesting stories... and it's extremely well written.

The Commanding Heights: The Battle for the World Economy

A good read on the 20th century's battle between free markets and central planning. The companion DVD set is excellent.

Churchill, Hitler, and "The Unnecessary War"

This great book exposes a lot of misconceptions about the "great statesman," Winston Churchill. You'll see how he drove the British Empire into the ground.

The Prize

An incredible history of oil, full of neat stories and facts. Daniel Yergin achieved something great by writing this book.